MOMENT OF TRUTH IN IRAQ

MOMENT
OF TRUTH
IN IRAQ

*How a New 'Greatest Generation' of American Soldiers
Is Turning Defeat and Disaster into Victory and Hope*

M I C H A E L   Y O N

RICHARD VIGILANTE BOOKS

PUBLISHED BY RICHARD VIGILANTE BOOKS

Copyright © 2008 by Michael Yon

All Rights Reserved

www.richardvigilantebooks.com

RVB with the portrayal of a Labrador retriever in profile is a trademark

of Richard Vigilante Books

Book design by Charles Bork

Library of Congress Control Number: 2008921478

Applicable BISAC Codes:

HIS027170   HISTORY / Military / Iraq War (2003–)

POL037000   POLITICAL SCIENCE / Political Freedom & Security / Terrorism

BIO008000   BIOGRAPHY & AUTOBIOGRAPHY / Military

ISBN 978-0-9800763-2-5

PRINTED IN THE UNITED STATES OF AMERICA

10 9 8 7 6 5 4 3 2 1

First Edition

For the soldiers and their families

Contents

MOMENT
OF TRUTH
IN IRAQ

CHAPTER ONE

Be Not Afraid

You shall cross the barren desert, but you shall not die of thirst.
You shall wander far in safety though you do not know the way.
You shall speak your words in foreign lands and all will understand.
You shall see the face of God and live.
Be not afraid. I go before you always;
Come follow me, and I will give you rest.

FROM A PRAYER CARD I FOUND ON A BASE IN ANBAR PROVINCE, IRAQ

• Baqubah, Iraq, June 19, 2007 •

Thoughts flow on the eve of a great battle. By the time you read these words, we will be in combat. Few ears have heard even rumors of this battle, and fewer still are the eyes that will see its full scope. Even now—for the battle has already begun for some—little news of it reaches home. I have known of the plans for a month, but have remained silent.

This campaign, a series of carefully orchestrated battalion- and brigade-sized operations, is collectively the largest battle since "major hostilities" ended more than four years ago. Even the media here on the ground do not seem to have sensed its scale.

Al Qaeda and associates had little or no presence in Iraq before the current war. But we made huge mistakes early on and now we pump blood and gold into the desert to pay for those blunders. We failed to secure the streets and we sowed doubt and mistrust. We disbanded the government and the army and we created a vacuum. We tolerated corruption and ineptitude and mostly local talent filled the ranks of an insurgency. But when we flattened parts of Fallujah not once but twice in response to the murders of four of our people, we helped create a spectacle of injustice and chaos. Al Qaeda took entrée while militias and insurgency groups began to thrive. The magnitude of true injustices was magnified line by line, hair by hair, by a frenzied media. But it wasn't the media's fault; the media did not flatten Fallujah or rape and torture the prisoners. We did that all by ourselves.

We walked into a dry, cracked land, along the two arteries of Mesopotamia that have long pulsed water and blood into the sea. In a place where everything that is not desert is tinder; sparks make fire.

When we devastated Fallujah, al Qaeda grew like a tumor. Before al Qaeda we faced a bewildering complex of insurgent groups with conflicting ideologies and goals, along with opportunistic thugs. The amalgam of men (and women) with guns was so diverse and the affiliations so dynamic that it was hard to track who was responsible for what atrocity. Each attack spawned reprisals that demanded yet another round of revenge. Al Qaeda had been trying to ignite a civil war here for several years; chaos and brutality would become its fuel.

Today al Qaeda is strong, but their welcome grows cold. The Coalition was not alone in failing to keep its promises. Iraqis love to say "America put a man on the moon but cannot turn on our lights," and the implication was we really didn't care. In so many ways we lost the moral high ground.

But then al Qaeda raped too many women and boys, cut off too many heads, and brought drugs into too many neighborhoods. And they haven't even *tried* to get the power going, or keep the markets open, or build schools, or playgrounds, or clinics for the children. Instead, as we ineptly tried to rebuild, they destroyed. They destroyed and murdered Iraqis who dared to work in such places or patronize them. And not only schools and clinics: they brought murder to mosques and churches too.

Finally, those few who were paying very close attention could feel it. It was there. A barely perceptible change in the atmosphere that signals big change could come. But to make the change we had to change. Remarkably we did. But that story is for later.

Just as this sentence was written, we began dropping bombs south of Baghdad and our troops are in contact.

In the context of this great campaign, the Battle of Baqubah, northeast of Baghdad, will be but one small part. But for those involved it will not seem small. Innocent civilians are being asked to leave. More than one thousand al Qaeda fighters are said to be in Baqubah, with perhaps another thousand adjuncts. Baqubah alone might be as intense as Operation Phantom Fury in Fallujah in late 2004.

They are ready for us. Giant bombs are buried in the roads. Snipers have chiseled holes in walls so that they can shoot not from roofs or windows, but from deep inside buildings, where we cannot see the flash or hear the shots. They will shoot for our faces and necks. Car bombs are already assembled. Suicide vests are prepared.

The enemy will try to herd us into their traps, and likely many of us will be killed before it ends. Already they have been blowing up bridges to restrict our movements. Entire buildings are rigged with explosives. They have rockets, mortars, and bombs hidden in places they know we are likely to cross, or to seek cover. They will use human shields and force people to drive bombs at us.

They will use their favorite of all weapons, the camera, and make it look like we are ravaging the city and that they are defeating us. For they have understood from the beginning what we learned almost too late: this is political war and political war is media war.

By the time this dispatch is published, we will be inside Baqubah, and we will be killing them.

Our jets will drop bombs. Helicopters will cover us and medevac our wounded and killed. Artillery will be firing, and our tanks moving in. And Humvees. And Strykers. Our people will capture commanding positions and cut off escape routes. The idea this time is not to chase al Qaeda out, but to trap and kill them head-on, or in ambushes, or while they sleep. This time, when they are wounded, they will be unable to go to hospitals without being captured, and so their wounds will fester and some will die painfully. It will be horrible for al Qaeda. Horror they sowed and tonight horror they will reap.

They will get no rest. No one is asking for surrender, but because we are who we are, if they surrender, they will be taken.

Our soldiers will go in on foot and fight from house to house. They will shoot rockets into enemy hiding spaces. Our snipers will shoot them in their heads and chests. All the talk of what should or could be done will smash head-on against the searing reality of combat.

Nothing is certain. I am here and have been all year. We are in trouble, but we have a great general. The only one, I have long believed, who can lead the way out of this morass. Iraq is not hopeless. Iraq can stand again, but first it must cast off these demons. Or kill them.

And while the battle rages, the prayer card will be in my pocket.

Be not afraid. I go before you always;
Come follow me, and I will give you rest.

CHAPTER TWO

Witness

I wrote the dispatch that became the previous chapter on the eve of Operation Arrowhead Ripper, one part of a great campaign to cast out of Iraq a demon we ourselves had done much to conjure. And though the battle, by the ordinary standards of battles, was a great victory, almost a year later the outcome is still in question. For this is a special kind of war; the kind in which we can win a battle or lose it, and not know which until the world sees it on the news. On one battlefield soldiers and civilians die. On another are shaped the images that define victory or defeat.

Combat is only one form of confrontation. I chose another.

This is how I became a witness to this war.

I grew up in Florida. Joined the army for college money and made it into Special Forces. The same week I graduated from Special Forces "selection," I was charged with murder after a fistfight in a Maryland nightclub. Those charges were eventually dropped, but the media coverage taught me to be wary of journalists. My first sharp lesson in the power of the press.

Special Forces gave me shelter, taught me to speak German, and tried to teach me Polish. After the army and college, I started a business in Poland. I saw firsthand the messy business of birthing democracy and toured the wreckage of Communism in Czechoslovakia, East Germany, and Romania. I learned that the only way to shackle hundreds of millions of people to a bankrupt ideology was to control the media. My second lesson in the power of the press.

I turned to writing and penned a book called *Danger Close*, published in 1999. Along the way, I learned the importance of images and took to the camera as well. Photographing birds in India, I stumbled across modern-day remnants of an ancient cult of cannibals who still conducted human sacrifice. I circled the globe six times to tease out their secrets.

Understanding the nuance of cult and the power of media would become essential tools for unraveling the tangled mess of myths and mysteries that obscure the Iraq War. From this distance I can see that before I went off the trail in search of cannibals and their cults, my journey into Iraq had already begun.

The trail of the cults took me from war-ravaged Nepal, where I talked with Maoist guerrillas; to Tibet, whose cults were only matched in number by its mystics; and to China, where the notion of a human collective seems to have achieved its greatest triumphs. Along the way I returned again and again to India. India is to cults as Switzerland is to watches and banking. I've had two lives: the life in India, and all the rest.

In early 2003, while I was infiltrating a cult in northern California, the Bush administration was doing the modern equivalent of a war dance. The other tribe was called Iraq. On the weekends I joined as witness to peace protests in San Francisco.

By March 19, 2003, I'd gained access to the cult and was living at their domicile. I was in their ashram in Sonoma while Coalition

Forces were rumbling into and over Iraq. At about midnight, I stepped into the cold and photographed what appeared to be a full moon overhead. The war had begun. The bullets were flying and bombs splitting the air. Saddam went into hiding; his army mostly melted away; the parts that stood were mostly destroyed.

I watched on television between meditations.

On May 1, George Bush declared "the end of major conflict."

That same month, the newly constituted Coalition Provisional Authority under Paul Bremer disbanded the Iraqi Army, abolished the ministries and institutions of Saddam's regime, and banned members of his Ba'ath party from holding positions in the new government.

Major combat ceased, they said. The enemy kept fighting. The war had hardly begun. In July, General John Abizaid conceded that U.S. forces were facing a classic guerrilla campaign.

On August 19, a huge suicide bomb destroyed the United Nations mission in Baghdad, killing at least twenty people and injuring more than one hundred, including UN envoy Sergio Vieira de Mello. Some six hundred surviving staffers left Iraq, and other (NGOs) non-governmental organizations moved out of Baghdad. The insurgents were doing a fine job of splitting the Coalition away from the people.

Ten days later another car bomb, in Najaf, killed Ayatollah Mohammed Baqr al Hakim and at least one hundred twenty-five other Shiites. Sunni insurgents were blamed for the attack, igniting ancient animosities that had been exploited but managed by Saddam. With the attack on the UN ensuring the Coalition would be the sole governing force in Iraq, the Najaf bombing may have been al Qaeda's first great strike in its campaign to fan those animosities into a civil war.

Within months our people faced a powerful, adaptive, and violent insurgency, without the tools to fight it.

The insurgency grew more lethal and persistently made the news, even when it meant kidnapping foreign nationals, including journalists, and filming their barbaric executions. These attacks undermined claims about how "weak" and "impotent" the insurgents were and raised doubts about the competence and veracity of American government leaders who had dismissed them. The attacks also sent many journalists packing and forced others to limit the scope of their coverage. Insurgency is political war. Imagine running a political campaign when the opponents own the media. Now imagine opponents with guns and bombs who kiss death for glory.

★   ★   ★

I was in Massachusetts when my old friend, Master Sergeant Richard L. Ferguson, died in a Humvee rollover on March 30, 2004, while conducting combat operations in Samarra, Iraq. "Fergy" was a fixture in the 10th Special Forces Group. I'd had lunch with him in Colorado shortly before he deployed to the war.

The next day a report from Fallujah showed a mob of Iraqis dancing and chanting as they mutilated four American security contractors. One of the mutilated bodies on the screen had been Scott Helvenston, ex-Navy SEAL and super-athlete with whom I'd gone to high school in Florida.

I flew to Colorado for Fergy's funeral, a gathering of family, friends, and comrades. They fired the guns, played Taps, and lowered Fergy into the soggy earth.

At the reception, soldiers kept telling me the media was not delivering an accurate story on Iraq and I should go there. "No thanks," was my stock answer. I hadn't written a word about the war and had no intention of starting.

From Colorado I flew to Florida for Scott's memorial. Media from as far away as Japan were camped in front of his mother's home, using telephoto lenses to try to get photos of the family through the blinds. Reporters stalked Scott's friends, lobbing their politically loaded questions and calling Scott a mercenary.

The media wasn't interested in Fergy's death. But the images of anti-American mobs dancing around the mutilated corpses of Scott and his comrades, broadcast around the world, brought the global media to my hometown.

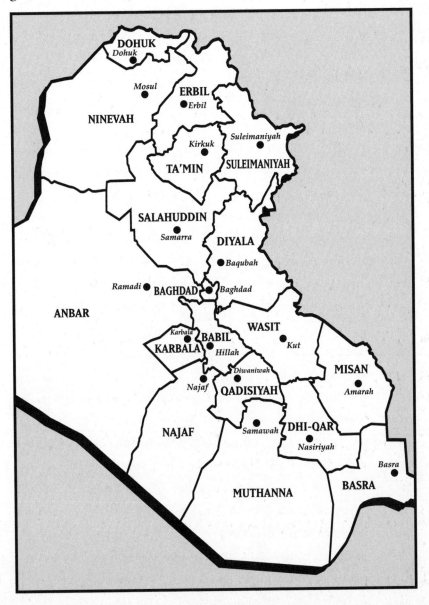

That month, April 2004, our military began wreaking havoc on Fallujah. Later in April, the prisoner-abuse scandals from Abu Ghraib hit the headlines. The pictures of abused prisoners became al Qaeda's best recruitment posters. Like the photo of the naked little girl running from her napalmed village in Vietnam, those images would become icons with profound implications for this war.

At home, many were bitter with the media for exposing Abu Ghraib. But it wasn't the press abusing prisoners for entertainment, and it wasn't the press that had taken the pictures. Seymour Hersch was one of the first to have broken the story, but Iraqis had known about it for a long time. The detainees returning home from our prisons abused and humiliated were all someone's father or brother or son or grandson. Keeping the American public in the dark would not change what the Iraqis knew.

Madison Avenue at its best could not have done more for al Qaeda and other insurgent groups than the flattening of Fallujah, or the Abu Ghraib photos. Abu Ghraib widened the gulf between our military and the worldwide media, not to mention that our forces are held to an incredibly high moral standard while the enemy is held to no standard. When the enemy sawed off a man's head on camera and posted the video online, it would be reported as evidence of our failure to protect civilians. Crimes against humanity committed by terrorists outside our control were blamed on the United States.

How could the U.S. military be such an outstanding fighting force—so good at all the other grim jobs of war—and be so politically dense and media-illiterate? My closest friends, people I would fight and die for, know less about the power of a photo than I know about sewing drapes.

The correlation of media, counterinsurgency, cult, and leadership seemed painfully obvious to me. Al Qaeda was a cult that had skillfully used our mistakes to make itself great among the people, while placing on us the ignominy of its own brutality.

That's when I began thinking that maybe I did have something to offer. By now, all I needed was a serious nudge. A childhood friend had grown up to become a lieutenant colonel who was in Tikrit. LTC Rodney Morris would e-mail and call sometimes, telling me that as a writer I should get to Iraq. I refused every entreaty. "It's your duty," he said. He knew which buttons to press, yet month after month I refused even to entertain the thought.

On November 7, 2004, just days after President Bush was re-elected, Operation Phantom Fury was launched. While our soldiers, marines and other Coalition members, kicked in Fallujah's front door, enemies old and new scrambled out the back, while others raced to Iraq. Four days later, the northern city of Mosul fell to terrorists when the Iraqi Police abandoned their stations. The scene all across Iraq was chaos: fighting was on a scale not seen since the invasion, and U.S. casualties were mounting. We were losing the war. The government was not telling the truth. I had learned from firsthand experience to be skeptical of the media. I contacted my old friend LTC Rodney Morris saying I was ready to come to Iraq.

Like most of the people who would later be called "alternate media," I bore all expenses personally, including travel and equipment. I had no media affiliation.

When I arrived in late December, the fighting in Baghdad was pitched and constant. Massive explosions and gunfire around the clock. My first impression was that the media had been too kind; Baghdad sounded like a free-fire zone. I did not know it then, but December 2004 would be one of the worst months for Baghdad during the entire war.

In late January 2005, as the date for Iraq's first post-invasion elections drew near, the media swarmed into Iraq to cover the predicted slaughters at polling stations. Instead, there were incredible turnouts. The press came to cover a funeral and stumbled into a baptism. I had been in Iraq little more than a month, and that month had been plenty eventful with lots of bullets and bombs, yet the incredible election persuaded me to stay a little longer, despite the smoldering body parts I had already seen.

When an entire press corps could be completely surprised by events happening in plain sight, something was fundamentally wrong with how the war was being reported. And fought.

Realizing no publication would likely print the unvarnished truth according to me, I started posting my dispatches on the Internet one week before the election.

Soon people were calling me a "blogger." Before I could figure out whether that was an insult or a compliment, my "traffic" was growing quickly.

By May, millions of people had seen my work. The mainstream press took notice. Some journalists sneered at my work. The most common criticism was that I lacked objectivity, because I called enemy fighters "terrorists" for murdering civilians, or I openly admitted that I hoped our side would win and Iraq would be free from dictatorship and terrorists.

I returned home after spending most of 2005 in the war, my ears still ringing from all the combat. I realized that after more than three years of fighting and more than two thousand U.S. troops killed in action Americans were losing patience. Meanwhile, Iraq was descending into such chaos and brutality that few bothered to complain about the paucity of reporting. Violence spiked in the last quarter of 2006. Democrats won control of both houses of Congress, largely because of voter frustration with the war.

We were getting close to the tipping point. The army had refused to let me back into the war, but after some media battles, they allowed me back in December 2006, as our country stood on the brink of defeat and Iraq gazed across the threshold of Hell. And then, at the very last moment, we stepped back from the edge. And the story changed. We came to the moment of truth.

Today, though that moment is not yet surely gained, it remains within our grasp as long as we are true to ourselves. For it is our values that can win this war, for us and for the Iraqi people, just as betraying those values very nearly lost it.

CHAPTER THREE

Walking the Line

During 2006, I traveled to Afghanistan and reported that the war there was going badly and deteriorating. Later in the year, the U.S. Army blocked my request to re-embed with U.S. forces in Iraq. An article published in *The Weekly Standard* titled "Censoring Iraq" changed the army's mind. Before returning to Iraq, there were the Killing Fields of Cambodia and war museums in northern Vietnam to visit, including the prison where now-senator John McCain and others had been held and tortured. Newspaper and magazine articles were displayed behind museum glass, the headlines strikingly similar to those framing the war in Iraq.

Then to Kuwait to tour critical support facilities, intending to publish a dispatch until the war interrupted. On to Qatar to tour other facilities, where I came across a Stryker that had been blown up over a year earlier in Mosul, which figured in a dispatch called "Angels Among Us." It was the *same* Stryker. All the soldiers who had been inside survived despite massive damage to the

Stryker, which after more than a year was nearly ready to return to combat.

★   ★   ★

On December 26, 2006, I flew back to Iraq from an airbase in Kuwait that is not secret, but whose name cannot be mentioned. A military bus took us to a C-17, a large cargo jet, squatting on the tarmac. A young U.S. Air Force loadmaster asked the bus passengers if they had any ammunition in their weapons. The soldiers were all armed, but their weapons were (presumably) cleared of ammo.

We walked onto the jet. No x-ray machine, no metal detectors, no tickets, or boarding passes. The flight was mostly empty, so we could sit where we wanted, strapping into two-point seatbelts on the canvas-and-metal bench seats. A crewman gave a quick tutorial in case of emergency—how to operate the oxygen masks, how to exit the craft after a crash landing, where to find an airsick bag—like on a commercial flight, but without the hula-hand gesturing. Combat soldiers actually pay attention to emergency briefings. A jet full of U.S. soldiers is probably one of the safest flights in the world, except that this C-17 was headed into Iraq.

During the flight I was allowed into the cockpit where one of the pilots said to take one of the two empty seats behind him. He demonstrated how to flip on the oxygen switch and don the mask. I buckled up and gazed out the windows at Iraq, miles below, and thought about what waited ahead this time.

Sometimes people ask me to "sum up" the strategic situation in Iraq. I prefer to write what I see with my own eyes in the streets and on the battlefield, to paint a picture as intimate and rich in detail as I can, and then, as much as possible, let the reader come to his own understanding. To "sum things up" generally means reporting second- or thirdhand, and although that can be an important thing to do, it's not what I do.

Within a few weeks of my trip back, however, a man whose firsthand knowledge of the war exceeds just about anyone's would offer this overview of conditions as of late 2006:

January 23, 2007
Opening Statement of General David Petraeus
before the Senate Armed Services Committee

Mr. Chairman, Senator McCain,
Members of the Committee:

Thank you for the opportunity to appear before you. I'd like to begin this morning by briefly reviewing the situation in Iraq, explaining the change in focus of the new strategy and discussing the way ahead. . . .

The situation in Iraq has deteriorated significantly since the bombing this past February of the Al-Askari Mosque in Samarra, the third-holiest Shia Islamic shrine.

The increase in the level of violence since then, fueled by the insurgent and sectarian fighting that spiraled in the wake of the bombing, has made progress in Iraq very difficult and created particularly challenging dynamics in the capital city of Baghdad.

Indeed, many Iraqis in Baghdad today confront life-or-death, stay-or-leave decisions on a daily basis. They take risks incalculable to us just to get to work, to educate their children, and to feed their families.

In this environment, Iraq's new government, its fourth in three and a half years, has found it difficult to gain traction. Though disappointing, this should not be a surprise. We should recall that after the liberation of Iraq in 2003, every governmental institution in the country collapsed. A society already traumatized by decades of Saddam's brutal rule was thrown into complete turmoil, and the effects are still evident throughout the country and in Iraqi society.

Iraq and its new government have been challenged by insurgents, international terrorists, sectarian militias, regional meddling, violent criminals, governmental dysfunction, and corruption. Iraq's security forces and new governmental institutions have struggled in this increasingly threatening environment, and the elections that gave us such hope actually intensified sectarian divisions in the population at the expense of the sense of Iraqi identity. In this exceedingly difficult situation, it has proven very hard for the new government to develop capacity and to address the issues that must be resolved to enable progress.

The escalation of violence in 2006 undermined the Coalition strategy and raised the prospect of a failed Iraqi state, an outcome that would be in no group's interest save that of certain extremist organizations and perhaps states in the region that wish Iraq and the United States ill. In truth, no one can predict the impact of a failed Iraq on regional stability, the international economy, the global war on terror, America's standing in the world, and the lives of the Iraqi people. . . .

★   ★   ★

Most of my first few weeks in Iraq during 2007 would confirm this grim assessment. But there was also something General Petraeus was well aware of but perhaps prudently did not stress before the Senate: our enemy had made mistakes far more devastating than our own, inadvertently opening a path to redemption for us as well as for Iraq.

As the C-17 began its descent, the pilot said I could stay in the cockpit. The crew was going to don body armor and the pilot said

I could wear it or not. I stepped down from the cockpit and returned wearing my body armor and my helmet. Behind the wide-open cockpit were passengers armed with assault weapons, pistols, and knives. Flight safety rules were very different here.

A journalist arriving in Baghdad has to make his or her way from the airport to the International Zone (the IZ or Green Zone), where the Combined Press and Information Center (CPIC) is located, to get credentials. Most journalists wait for the Rhino—basically an armored shuttle between the airport and the International Zone. The wait is usually a long one—the runs are infrequent and unscheduled. The credentials could easily be issued in Kuwait, and the silly and unnecessary trip into and out of the IZ can cost journalists several days, depending on the breaks. For a television crew with several people, the wasted time easily translates into tens of thousands of dollars in direct cost and lost opportunity just to pick up little plastic badges. The journalists pace about in waiting rooms, voices pitched with frustration, telling editors in London or Denver, "We'll have to cancel the trip to Balad. There is no way around it. Four days to get badges." Serious journalists understand and accept the hassles organic to covering war. But they also factor in these synthetic hassles and wasted days and dollars before coming to Iraq. The inauspicious entrée to the war can set a foul tone even for the most fair-minded. If after five years at war, a plastic badge with a photo and fingerprint requires days of wasted time, what's happening with the *rest* of the war?

While a group of journalists hunkered down for the next Rhino, I headed for Catfish Air to book a helicopter flight that would leave in minutes. Once aboard, the helicopter pilots switched off their lights and zoomed low over Baghdad. Baghdad was well lit, albeit mostly by private generators, as the city power pulsed only part of each day.

At CPIC was a German professor named Dietmar Herz. Planning to embed only briefly, Professor Herz had been stuck there for five days, a prisoner of bureaucratic inertia and his polite reluctance to make a nuisance of himself. Every journalist needs to have body armor, a helmet, ballistic glasses, and flame-retardant gloves. Professor Herz didn't have any gloves. I didn't want to read about his death only to wonder if flame-retardant gloves would have made the difference between escape and cremation, so I gave him my extra pair.

I wasted only one day getting the badge. Journalists who embed for only a of couple weeks can plan on about ten completely wasted days getting in and out, and so a two-week embed nets usually less than five harried and nearly useless days. The next morning, leaving Professor Herz to languish at CPIC, I met up with Command Sergeant Major Jeffrey Mellinger, the senior-enlisted soldier in Iraq. CSM Mellinger was the right-hand man of the top general in Iraq, making Mellinger premier non-commissioned officer for every enlisted person—be they army, air force, navy, or marine. This also included all Coalition members such as the Poles, the Estonians, Koreans, and all the rest. In 2005, I'd learned there was no better way to get a clear read of events in Iraq than shadowing CSM Mellinger around Iraq as he walked the line.

CSM Mellinger had more access to Iraq and the entire theatre than nearly anyone. Access that included every guard tower, secret chamber, and ditch, and anywhere else U.S. or Coalition forces might be in Iraq, Kuwait, Jordan, or even out on ships in the Gulf. Mellinger earned an iconic status among young soldiers, because he popped up in every remote and dangerous corner, from mailrooms to maintenance bays, hospitals to police stations, combat missions and full-on firefights to memorials.

On two separate occasions I photographed CSM Mellinger changing his own flat Humvee tires, fully exposed on dangerous roads north of Baghdad. He didn't ask anybody to do anything he wouldn't do, and so he served the equivalent of two back-to-back tours, and then half of another tour on top of that, without a break other than normal leave.

Mellinger, with about thirty-five years of continuous military service, was a draftee. Tell him the American military is an "all volunteer army," and he'll shoot back, "Like hell it is."

One young sergeant, a team member on CSM Mellinger's crew, told me their team had already been attacked twenty-six times. When I asked Mellinger, he shrugged and said, "Sounds about right." Five of his Humvees had been destroyed by IEDs; he was riding in two of those when the bombs exploded, yet nobody in his crew was ever seriously wounded. Experience multiplied by luck. I have not met another soldier who understands the battlefields of Iraq better than Jeff Mellinger, and I used to tell him he should be on every morning show in America. But Mellinger was right where he wanted to be.

★   ★   ★

Soon after we met up in December 2006, CSM Mellinger said something I hadn't heard yet. When I had landed at Baghdad International Airport (BIAP), Saddam Hussein was in a cell somewhere nearby, his execution imminent.

Saddam had been convicted and sentenced to death, but only a few people knew when the execution would be carried out. On the eve of the hanging, while we were having dinner with troops in Anbar province, Mellinger delivered the news in a "no-room-for-BS-talk," the only kind combat soldiers will tolerate.

There was a time when Saddam believed that the desert heat would prove too much for pampered American soldiers. There was a time when Saddam's own subordinates were afraid to openly disagree with him. His bully class ruled through murder and fear.

His Iraq had been at civil war, or at war with its neighbors, long before most Americans could find it on a map.

There was a time when he used chemical weapons on humans. There was a time when he set Kuwait's oil wells ablaze in a tantrum, poisoning the earth, the air, and the sea. If he couldn't have them, he'd make sure no one else could either, and he was willing to poison the globe.

When Saddam was driven into hiding by the same soldiers he'd once called weak, he crawled into a hole in the ground to avoid capture just outside of his hometown Tikrit, not far from where he is buried now.

Saddam Hussein Abd al-Majid al-Tikriti never denied being a mass murderer. He never apologized for it. He never showed any inclination to mend his ways. Judging from the violent and suspiciously timed deaths of a series of lawyers and judges assigned to his trial, his hands were never washed clean.

As Saddam was led up the scaffold's steps, someone used a cell phone to record the affair. The noose was slipped around his neck. The trapdoor swung open and his body fell to the end of the rope, his weight wrenched a giant gash in his neck as his body jerked to a swinging halt. His soul kept going.

When the hanging sentence was issued, speculation mounted about the likelihood of massive Sunni reprisals when Saddam was executed. Like other forecasts of imminent catastrophe—the predictions of large-scale terrorist attacks disrupting the first Iraqi elections—the Sunni uprising didn't happen. Few cried for Saddam Hussein.

★   ★   ★

As I toured with CSM Mellinger in the following weeks, I saw firsthand the war of attrition our troops faced: roadside bombs, rockets, mortars, and small-arms fire were part of a violent landscape. Insurgent attacks resulted in almost daily casualties.

In late 2006, nowhere were these dangers more menacing than in Anbar province. Anbar is a vast, often lawless frontier stretching west from near Baghdad to the Syrian border. The population is almost exclusively Sunni Arab, leaving little cause for sectarian violence but plenty of other reasons to fight.

Major cities in Anbar, such as Fallujah, were fantastically dangerous in late 2006. Yet the U.S. Marines and Army, along with some U.S. Navy and Air Force personnel, were probably stretched as thin here as the U.S. Border Patrol between the U.S. and Mexico. No matter how they spread it, our fighters simply did not have enough paint to cover the barn. Americans normally put at least two people per guard position, but in Anbar—where the fighting was brutal—I saw places where they had only one.

Hidden bombs could take America's toughest tank—the mighty M1, weighing in at roughly one hundred fifty thousand pounds—and heave it into the air, sending its heavy turret sailing a hundred yards and flipping the rest of the burning hulk on its back like a giant, exploding turtle. When such bombs detonated under Humvees, the scattered remnants might fit into the trunk of another Humvee. Smaller IEDs (improvised explosive devices) and EFPs (explosive formed projectiles) ripped through the vehicles like cannonballs through fog, leaving dusty, mud-cratered roads looking like the moon.

The provincial capital of Anbar, Ramadi, was the location for several stops on CSM Mellinger's patrol. The enemy snipers there have become good and even excellent. Just during the time we were in the area, they killed four of our people. Baghdad and other places surely were dangerous, but Anbar was worse in every measure, and Ramadi was the worst place in Anbar, which explained why CSM Mellinger kept going there.

Bombs and bullets were often taking several marines or soldiers per day, along with many others wounded, but the increasing depravity of the enemy was hurting the enemy more than us. At some point in the journey, CSM Mellinger informed me that Iraqi forces had just captured one of the perpetrators involved in a recent high-profile ambush of American soldiers. Two soldiers had been captured, tortured, murdered, and mutilated. The enemy then rigged the bodies with explosives. I could write many pages about the depravity of the enemies in Iraq.

The Measure of Morale

As I traveled around with CSM Mellinger, I watched for signs of the state of morale in the face of these horrors. Gauging morale is not a simple affair of asking a few soldiers how they are feeling today. Happy soldiers may complain loudly, while profoundly depressed, demoralized, and angry ones might stay quiet. A person must live with them and keep eyes and ears open for a range of signs. High-morale troops are disciplined and focused on the mission. Troops with high morale are usually friendly and polite to strangers. They keep their quarters neat and their weapons clean. When they're not out in the field, they drill and practice and learn new skills to keep their edge.

Bad morale reveals itself through apathy. Soldiers might be quiet and sullen. When they do speak, it's often in argument. They neglect the mission and focus on their own needs and feelings. They become petty, complain about small problems, and become risk-averse. They find ways to look like they're doing their job instead of doing it.

Mail is more important than even hot showers or hot food. When I was in Fallujah, the mail center received about eight shipping containers every two days; three were filled with letters. People at home probably have no idea how much their little cards, letters, and goodie bags boost morale. Countless walls around Iraq are wallpapered with cards and letters. Soldiers and marines especially love the cards from kids. There is nothing better over here than reading two-dozen cards from kids who can barely hold a crayon. If a kid sends a card, rest assured that card will be stuck on a wall somewhere, and it will bring a smile to many a soldier and marine.

A dog is instant morale. The army prohibits soldiers from adopting dogs, but I have yet to visit a base where combat soldiers or marines did not keep dogs, often secretly. The Tennessee National Guard kept so many dogs that some of them slept right outside the primitive dining facility and were too lazy to roll over. But at night those dogs were along the perimeter, barking at anyone who approached. The "Deuce Four" Battalion up in Mosul adopted a dog named Sheba, who one day brought the heart of a suicide bomber to the soldiers. When "vector control" people later tried to take Sheba away, the battalion commander refused and warned them never to come back. Deuce Four soldiers said that Sheba alerted them to threats several times. Sheba has since retired happily to Colorado with a Deuce Four soldier.

Humor is the key sign. I saw a Christmas tree in Anbar decorated with bullets. A sergeant told me that a soldier had used a grenade for an ornament. Apparently that was a little over the top even for Anbar province, and so hand grenades were removed from the list of acceptable Christmas decorations. When I saw a snowman holding a sign that said, "Will Work for Crack," I knew morale was high.

Folks at home might never have guessed from the news, but it was clear as I walked the line with CSM Mellinger, that morale among American and Iraqi forces all over the country ranged from good to high. Made me wonder what they knew that most Americans didn't. (However, later in 2007, I was seeing isolated places were morale was flagging, and the soldiers wanted me to write about it; the long and back-to-back tours were ripping their families apart. Retired General Barry McCaffrey had told me, and he had written on numerous occasions, that our military was too small. During 2007, I would see firsthand that he was right, though in general, morale—seemingly miraculously—remains at least good.)

Combat soldiers have little patience for less than unvarnished truth. That's why I spend so much time with infantry. Worst job in the world—not "cool" like Special Operations Forces—but devoid of pretense. Lots of straight talk in small words.

A combat soldier seldom says a word if a grunt will do. They post signs like "Watch out for dumbass camels," and "DON'T PUT YOUR SHIT HERE," with an arrow pointing to the floor. They say things like, "Don't stand up on this roof, because you'll get shot," instead of, "The security situation in Ramadi is tenuous, and so visitors are advised to wear helmets in the case of some untoward event or happenstance that might occur in a combat zone." No, infantry signs say: "The last dumbass who didn't duck got shot in the head." After a year away, I found the plain talk bracing and encouraging. It boosted my morale.

The U.S. soldiers were not out to capture terrorists but to kill them, though they captured far more than they killed, and gleaned great information from them. And they would say it: *We are here to kill the terrorists.* Even in January 2007, when the common sentiment back home was that the war was already lost (missing only that last scene of the last helicopter taking off from the embassy roof, desperate Iraqis clinging to the landing gear), most American soldiers continued to tell me they were winning despite the chaos and continuing losses. No matter what anyone might think of the strategy and tactics, straight talk is easy to understand. Being around the soldiers was an antidote to the malaise back home.

The troops weren't brainwashed or naïve. They often talked openly about what they thought of certain commanders or even the president, and this was especially true of the more rustic souls that I liked to talk with.

"Why don't that bastard for a president get hisself over here an' see for hisself we ain't got enough boots on th' groun'?"

"Are you saying we are losing?"

"Naw, I'm jus sayin' we need more boots. You know better 'n anyone that we kicks ass."

"Yes, I do. They are talking about bringing in more soldiers."

"Well, is 'bout time! I don' believe 'em, do you?"

"I'll believe it when I see them rolling up from Kuwait."

"Tha's what I'm talkin' 'bout."

CHAPTER FOUR

Mosul the Mirror

After our tour in Anbar province, we headed back to Baghdad before making the long and dangerous Humvee trip up to Mosul, where we arrived on January 3, 2007. I had spent the better part of five months there, starting in April 2005, when the fighting was furious.

Located in northern Iraq, straddling the Tigris River and close to the peaceful Kurdish Zone, Mosul is the capital city of Nineveh province. It is the second largest city in Iraq—unless you ask someone from Basra—and is ethnically rich with Arabs, Kurds, Turkomen, Assyrians, and Yezidis. And of course, Sunni, Shia, and Christian. Mosul has the highest proportion of Christians of all the Iraqi cities.

Mosul is an ancient place. Local legend says the prophet Jonah is buried in one of the city's mosques. Yet Mosul is home to one of the largest educational and research centers in the Middle East and the University of Mosul, College of Medicine is the second oldest medical college in Iraq. It is also home to many of Saddam's former military officers, tens of thousands of whom found themselves unemployed when the Iraqi Army was disbanded in 2003. Saddam's sons Uday and Qusay were killed in Mosul in July 2003, a few months after then two-star General David Petraeus led the 101st Airborne into Nineveh, rapidly turning the area into one of the conspicuous success stories of the war.

During the initial invasion of Iraq in March 2003, while some old-school commanders stormed into cities and towns across the country and crushed anything that dared resist, the Screaming Eagles of Petraeus's 101st shifted ingeniously from a kinetic force-on-force mode to a sort of "pre-counterinsurgency." As it swept up through Iraq, fighting in Karbala, Hilla, and Najaf, before launching one of the the longest and largest heliborne air assaults in history to reach Nineveh province—the 101st used masterful strokes, punching when needed, yet pulling punches that other leaders likely would have thrown.

In the days immediately following the invasion, Mosul had been taken almost without a fight by Kurdish Pershmerga and U.S. Special Forces, but the city quickly slid into anarchy and widespread looting ensued. Marines who came to restore order killed about fifteen people during two days of rioting and street fighting. When Petraeus took over this powder keg on April 22, he knew there was scant time before it exploded.

"An army of liberation has a certain shelf life," Petraeus reminded his troops, "before it becomes an army of occupation." His goal was to restore security and essential services and turn control over to the Iraqis as quickly as possible. The military action had to convey the political message: We're here to give you your country back and help you keep it. Counterinsurgency is political war. And though clever, cynical people like to say politics is about perception, Lincoln's wisdom about what percentage of the people you can fool what percentage of the time remains in force. Politics is not driven by perception for long, but by trust. It is not enough for the message to be pleasing; it must be true.

Mosul is home to so many retired Iraqi military that occupying the place was a little like a foreign army taking over Cumberland County, North Carolina, home of Fort Bragg and Pope AFB. There were many folks in Mosul who knew how to make trouble if so inclined. One of the first things Petraeus did was to meet with about forty local retired Iraqi generals.

After the first meeting, Petraeus saw those ex-generals every Tuesday for tea. With their support, Iraqi Police returned to their stations and began joint patrols with 101st soldiers. Between looting and closed borders, supplies in Mosul were running dangerously low. Petraeus worked with local leaders to reopen the borders and restore the flow of goods into Mosul. The economy began to reopen.

Petraeus organized elections so quickly Mosul's newly elected mayor was on the job before Coalition Provisional Authority Chief Paul Bremer arrived in Baghdad. Petraeus formed a governing council made up of local leaders representing all ethnic, tribal, and professional groups to restore government services. At the suggestion of one of his soldiers, the 101st put on a "Sheik Fest" as a way to get to know local tribal leaders.

In the fall of 2003, *New York Times* reporter Michael Gordon wrote that in Nineveh province the "American military, not the civilian-led occupation authority based in Baghdad, are the driving force in the region's political and economic reconstruction." He credited Petraeus, saying the general treated "nation-building as a central military mission" and was "prepared to act while the civilian authority in Baghdad was still getting organized."

Petraeus improvised a series of civic affairs initiatives, based on what he'd learned about local priorities and concerns from the sheiks, the Iraqi generals, and the local governing council. Projects ranged from putting frozen Iraqi funds into circulation to broadcasting a local news program on television. When some Iraqis voiced concerns that the night-vision goggles worn by U.S. soldiers could see through women's clothing, another officer in the 101st got the idea of organizing an informal meeting so local leaders could try the goggles themselves.

Signs in Coalition bases asked, "We are in a race to win over the people. What have you and your element done today to contribute to victory?" Petraeus instructed soldiers who conducted cordon and search operations to tell local residents, "Thank you for letting us search your house." As *Times* reporter Gordon noted, one natural advantage Petraeus and the 101st had was that as an airborne unit the division had lots of infantry soldiers "to conduct foot patrols and stay in touch with the local population." Petraeus commented, "We walk, and walking has a quality of its own." In Mosul, said the general, the soldiers of the 101st were "like cops on the beat." Counterinsurgency experts often compare urban counterinsurgency to community policing. In both cases the essential message is the same: "We are with you. What you value we value. Our strength is your strength." In both cases, it begins to work when the citizens join their strength to ours. The point is not merely to create warm fuzzies among the population but to enroll them in the fight, not by waging gun battles, but by passing the word and leaving the enemy no place to hide.

One of the locals' biggest concerns in Mosul was getting the university open again so the seventeen thousand students could complete the academic year. Under Saddam, only members of his Ba'ath Party could hold civil service jobs. Now the administration's de-Ba'athification program barred those very same people from any government agency. Result: not enough qualified instructors or administrators to run the university. Petraeus was able to win a suspension of that rule until the end of the academic year. The university and other agencies started functioning.

Petraeus succeeded in Mosul by acting quickly, forcefully, and adroitly to encourage cooperation from key local leaders. Elsewhere too many commanders spent that time waiting for instructions. Too many of our too few soldiers were sidelined, herded onto bases, and isolated from the populace by their commanders' indecision, while the political situation degenerated and unguarded weapon depots were being looted.

When the Coalition did finally make some decisions and assert itself, the result was disastrous. Tragically even in Mosul, the civil fabric Petraeus had knitted together began to unravel. Bremer, instructed by Washington, remained fanatic on the question of drumming ex-Ba'athists out of any civil service position. When the compromises negotiated by Petraeus expired, many of the ex-professors and administrators at Mosul University lost their jobs permanently. The retired and disenfranchised military—who had helped keep the growing insurgency at bay—were now told they wouldn't be part of the new Iraq, in direct contradiction to promises made by commanders on the ground. The most able and dangerous men in the country learned they could not trust American military commanders. Trust, the first and most important hill on the moral high ground, and we had abandoned it. Unable to support their families, cut off from their own country's future, furious at the new regime that had made them pariahs, these men were an insurgency waiting to happen. They did not wait for long.

As the discontent of dangerous men fed the growing violence, the Mosul economy deteriorated along with the security situation. As the violence spread, Petraeus acted quickly and decisively to restore order. But the very need to do so showed how much that had been gained was already slipping away.

Petraeus's successes in Nineveh were later the subject of a

Kennedy School of Government case study titled "The Accidental Statesman." But a sad epilogue to that study described the situation during Petraeus's last months in Mosul this way: "Although the situation had been difficult in early December 2003, by January 2004, the 101st Airborne had—through a series of aggressive but targeted raids—restored order. The worst appeared to be over; the 101st lost no soldiers for a month. . . . The Commanders Emergency Response Program (CERP) funds had begun to flow again following congressional action, and the 101st continued to put them to good use. In a flurry of activity in the weeks leading up to departure, the division oversaw the renovation or creation of a judicial center, a major corrections facility, a refinery, oil storage facilities, a joint security center, and the Village of Hope (for homeless families)."

The 101st turned over responsibility for Mosul to Task Force Olympia on February 5, 2004. The division headed home; Petraeus began his second tour in Iraq. This time he was charged with overseeing the training of Iraqi Security Forces, a job he described as "trying to drive a herd of cattle through a storm at night while getting shot at."

During 2005, as I watched simultaneously great progress with the development of the Iraqi Security Forces, for example, but also Iraq's collapse into chaos and civil war, I found the accounts— from both Americans and Iraqis—of what Petraeus and the 101st had accomplished in Nineveh amazing. But as Iraqis from all walks would later complain to me, Petraeus and the 101st had left too early. Most of the approximate twenty thousand soldiers of the 101st were out by early spring of 2004, leaving Nineveh to be covered by a force less than half that size. In November 2004, when Operation Phantom Fury pushed terrorists out of Fallujah, many of them fled to Mosul and Baqubah. Mosul fell as the Iraqi Police abandoned their stations under attack by terrorists.

American forces immediately took back the stations. But a

month later, in December 2004, a terrorist slipped into the dining facility on Forward Operating Base Marez, then, as now, the Army's main operating base in the city. The terrorist detonated his explosives vest during a crowded holiday meal, killing twenty-two and wounding another seventy-two. To the enemy the main value of such an attack, as always, was the propaganda coup. Images of the shattered mess hall played over and over in local media, making it appear that U.S. forces were being pushed around—and at a critical moment. Iraq's first national elections were scheduled for January 2005, only a month away. With the attack, Iraqi and American authorities actually gave some thought to canceling the elections, which would have been an even bigger PR disaster.

Enemy dominance of the media battle space translated quite directly into military setbacks. Terrorists from many countries swarmed into Iraq to be part of the victory they saw happening on their TV screens. And with Iraqis both enraged at U.S. conduct of the war in places like Fallujah, and at the same time terrified that U.S. and Iraqi Army forces could not protect them, al Qaeda in Iraq grew faster than bamboo in a rainforest.

From November 2004 on, the fighting in Mosul was constant, kinetic, and intense.

Combat Outpost Tampa (COP) in Mosul was manned by a platoon of the 1-24 Infantry Battalion known as the Deuce Four. On December 29, 2004, the post was nearly flattened by a huge truck bomb followed by a massive attack. For hours the terrorists brought more car bombs, IEDs, mortars, rockets, and massive amounts of small-arms fire. Even our pilots later told me they thought the Deuce Four platoon below was about to be wiped out. One pilot was directly over the initial truck bomb; the mushroom cloud was so large that he swerved his jet thinking it might affect his machine. Down below the pilots could see terrorists from multiple locations converging on the dazed American platoon, many of whom were wounded from the initial blast. The jets fired Phoenix missiles and ran strafing runs so low that one F-14 nearly crashed. Straining to catch radio calls from Deuce Four, the pilots could hardly hear the soldiers through the unceasing gunfire.

Were it not for one young Deuce Four soldier, Oscar Sanchez, who had fired at the initial truck bomb until it exploded prematurely, we might have lost another forty soldiers in the opening moments of the attack. If not for Oscar Sanchez, the platoon might well have been wiped out. If not for Oscar Sanchez, the elections might have been canceled. Oscar died in the blast.

Ultimately the Deuce Four, led by Lieutenant Colonel Erik Kurilla, fought off the attackers, apparently killing a couple dozen of them. LTC Kurilla sent the same platoon of tough soldiers that had held off the attack back to rebuild and reoccupy COP Tampa while their ears were still ringing. I would get to know Kurilla and the Deuce Four well when I embedded with them for about five months, starting that April, so the story didn't surprise me when I heard it later.

As always the enemy was fighting for the media battle space. The bad guys had filmed the attack from at least three angles (that I got hold of). For that very reason, the Deuce Four's resilience was crucial. Despite the enemy's media win, this was where the local tide started to turn, because the locals saw the Deuce Four reoccupy the shattered building and had seen the terrorists get their hearts ripped out in that battle.

The Deuce Four fought hard for a year, Kurilla's unit suffering about twenty-five percent killed or wounded out of a battalion of roughly seven hundred. On my first mission with them in April 2005, they lost two soldiers and one interpreter in a suicide car bomb attack. But for a year they dealt out far more punishment than they took. The Deuce Four was one of the worst things that could have happened to terrorists, crushing the enemy on all fronts, including the media battle space.

Every time Erik Kurilla killed or captured some bad guys (which was often when the Deuce Four was in Mosul in 2004–2005) he would say things like, "Every time we kill one of these smart cockroaches, they replace him with a lesser cockroach, and they get easier to kill." And boy, were they killing cockroaches. A cult began to grow around Deuce Four, especially among the Iraqi Police, Iraqi Army, and interpreters who traded stories of their courageous exploits alongside the American warriors who wore the emblem of the Punisher, and painted it onto buildings where they had killed terrorists.

LTC Kurilla's soldiers related an incident that occurred before I arrived in April 2005, when he or his guys killed an enemy one day, and the dead guy's cell phone rang. Kurilla's interpreter answered it. It was the dead guy's brother. The story goes that Kurilla said through the interpreter that he was the American commander, adding, "I just killed your brother and am coming to kill you!" A story like that only had to have a grain of truth to radiate through the Iraqi forces, generating respect for the Americans and reflected glory for themselves. Kurilla often used captured cell phones to disrupt enemy plans and to identify who was helping support the terror network. The ever-adaptive enemy attempted to reverse the advantage in this area through attacks on cell towers and very public and permanent punishment of civilians who were caught using cell phones, but their gain was only temporary. In 2007, I heard more than one American commander refer to his cell phone as his chief weapon against al Qaeda.

The Deuce Four used the media and mind games to unravel the enemy. One day the Deuce Four faked an IED attack using an Iraqi Security Force truck as the "target," complete with explosives and flash-bang grenades to simulate the IED. They even simulated evacuating casualties using sand-filled dummies.

The enemy took the bait. Terrorists came out and started with the AK-rifle-monkey-pump, shooting into the truck, their own video crews capturing the moment of glory. That's when the American snipers (Navy SEALs) opened fire and killed terrorists who were carrying weapons. For obvious reasons the great AK-monkey-pumpers smack-down was kept secret for a long time, until, with permission, I published it in the summer of 2005.

On August 18, 2005, just as the Deuce Four's deployment was about to end, the commander, LTC Erik Kurilla, became the 181st and last casualty.

That morning Deuce Four Sergeant Daniel Lama had been shot in the neck while on operations in downtown Mosul around Yarmook Traffic Circle, which terrorists had made probably the most dangerous traffic circle in the world. Daniel Lama was OK. But Kurilla gets upset when someone unrelated to the events called up a soldier's family and scared the life out of them with a "your son got shot but he's still alive" phone call. So the commander would always go to the combat support hospital, get the straight scoop from the doctors and the soldier (if he was conscious), and then Kurilla would call the family himself. Sometimes the commander was delivering bad news, other times he was just telling about near misses and concussions from car bombs, for instance, but at least it was accurate, and he would keep updating the family.

And so that morning, the commander rushed to the Combat Support Hospital, with Command Sergeant Robert Prosser along with his Iridium satellite phone. After calling Lama's mother to tell her Daniel got shot but he was OK, Kurilla led the men of the Deuce Four out to find the shooters. I rode in Kurilla's Stryker.

Hearing reports of automatic weapons fire back at Yarmook

Circle, we headed in that direction when LTC Kurilla spotted three men in a black Opal; Kurilla's sixth sense had become legendary that year and that sixth sense alerted on those men. The chase was on. Strykers are fast, but no match for an Opal downtown. The car likely would have escaped us were it not for the Kiowa Warrior helicopters working with us.

After some exciting car chase scenes, the Kiowa swooped low and a pilot leaned out with an M-4 rifle and fired on the Opal. The armed men abandoned the car and fled on foot. Our ramp dropped. We ran into combat. Urban combat. Chasing wild men into the labyrinth, soldiers enter the land of confusion.

There were shops, alleys, doorways, windows.

The soldiers with LTC Kurilla were searching fast, weapons at the ready, and they quickly found and flex-cuffed two men they thought might be the right guys. They weren't. Meanwhile, Deuce Four SSG Konkol and another squad were clearing toward us, leaving the three real bad guys boxed, but free.

Shots were fired behind us, but around a corner to the left.

A young second lieutenant and a young specialist who had joined Kurilla's crew that day were inside a shop when a close-quarters firefight broke out, and they ran outside. Not knowing how many men they were fighting, they wanted backup. LTC Kurilla began running in the direction of the shooting. He passed by me, and I chased, Kurilla leading the way.

There was a quick and heavy volume of fire. And then LTC Kurilla was shot. Kurilla was running while he was hit—in three places, including his femur which was shattered. The commander didn't seem to miss a stride. He did a crazy judo roll and came up shooting from a sitting position.

BamBamBamBam! Bullets were hitting all around Kurilla. The young second lieutenant and specialist who were part of Kurilla's crew that day were the only two soldiers nearby. Neither had real combat experience. Our interpreter, "A. H.," had no weapon. I had a camera.

Seconds count.

Kurilla, though down and unable to move, was fighting and firing, yelling at the two young soldiers to get in there, but they hesitated. BamBamBamBam!

Kurilla was in the open, but his judo roll had left him slightly to the side of the shop. I screamed to the young soldiers, "Throw a grenade in there!" but they were not attacking.

"Throw a grenade in there!" They did not attack.

"Give me a grenade!" They didn't have grenades.

"Erik! Do you need me to come get you!?" I shouted. But he said "No." (Thank God—running in front of the shop might have proved fatal.)

"What's wrong with you!?" I yelled above the shooting.

"I'm hit three times! I'm shot three times!"

Amazingly, he was right. One bullet smashed through his femur, snapping his leg. His other leg was hit and so was an arm.

With his leg mangled, Kurilla pointed and fired his rifle into the doorway, yelling instructions to the soldiers about how to get in there. But they were not attacking. This was not the Deuce Four I know. The other Deuce Four soldiers would have killed every man in that room in about five seconds. But these two soldiers didn't have the combat experience to grasp the power of momentum.

This was happening in seconds. Several times I nearly ran over to Kurilla, but hesitated. Kurilla was, after all, still fighting. And I was afraid to run in front of the shop, especially so unarmed.

And then help arrived in the form of one man: Command Sergeant Major Prosser.

Prosser ran around the corner, passed the two young soldiers who were crouched low, then by me and right to the shop, where he started firing at men inside.

A man came forward trying to shoot Kurilla with a pistol, apparently realizing his only escape was by fighting his way out, or dying in the process. Kurilla was aiming at the doorway waiting for him to come out. Had Prosser not come at that precise moment, who knows what the outcome might have been?

Prosser shot the man at least four times with his M-4 rifle. But the American M-4 rifles are weak—after Prosser landed three nearly point-blank shots in the man's abdomen, splattering a testicle with a fourth, the man just staggered back, regrouped, and tried to shoot Prosser.

Then Prosser's M-4 went "black" (no more bullets). A shooter inside was also having problems with his pistol, but there was no time to reload. Prosser threw down his empty M-4, ran into the shop, and tackled the man.

Though I have the photo, I do not remember the moment that Prosser went "black" and ran into the shop. Apparently I turned my head, but kept my finger on the shutter button. When I looked back again, I saw the very bloody leg of CSM Prosser inside the shop. It was not moving. He appeared to be shot down and dead.

I looked back at the two soldiers who were with me outside and screamed what amounted to "Attack! Attack! Attack!" I stood up and was yelling at them. Actually, what I shouted was an unprintable string of curses, while Kurilla was also yelling at them to get in there, his M-4 trained on the entrance. But the guys were not attacking.

I saw Prosser's M-4 on the ground. I picked it up. It was empty. I saw only Prosser's bloody leg lying still, just inside the darkened doorway, because most of his body was hidden behind a stack of sheet metal.

"Give me some ammo! Give me a magazine!" I yelled, and the young second lieutenant handed over a full 30-round magazine. I jacked it in, released the bolt, and hit the forward assist. I had only one magazine so checked that the selector was on semi-automatic.

I ran back to the corner of the shop and looked at LTC Kurilla who was bleeding, and saw CSM Prosser's extremely bloody leg inside the shop; the rest of him was still obscured from view. I was going to run into the shop and shoot every man with a gun. And I was scared to death.

What I didn't realize was at that same moment four soldiers from Alpha Company 2nd Platoon were arriving on scene, just in time to see me about to go into the shop. SSG Gregory Konkol, SGT Jim Lewis, and specialists Nicholas Devereaux and Christopher Muse were right there, behind me, but I didn't see them.

Reaching around the corner, I fired three shots into the shop. The third bullet pierced a propane canister, which jumped up in the air and began spinning violently. It came straight at my head but somehow missed, flying out of the shop as a high-pressure jet of propane hit me in the face. The goggles saved my eyes. I gulped in deeply.

In the tiniest fraction of a second, somehow my mind actually registered propane—FIREBALL! as it bounced on the ground where it spun furiously, creating an explosive cloud of gas and dust, just waiting for someone to fire a weapon.

I scrambled back, got up and ran a few yards, afraid that Kurilla was going to burn up if there was a fire. The soldiers from Alpha Company were heading toward him when LTC Kurilla yelled out that he was OK, but that CSM Prosser was still in the shop. The Alpha Company soldiers ran through the propane and dust cloud and swarmed the shop.

When the bullet hit that canister, Prosser—who I thought might be dead because of all the blood on his leg—was actually fighting hand-to-hand on the ground. Wrapped in a ground fight, Prosser could not pull out his service pistol strapped on his right leg, or get to his knife on his left, because the terrorist—who turned out to be a serious terrorist—had grabbed Prosser's helmet and pulled it over his eyes and twisted it.

Prosser had beaten the terrorist in the head three times with his fist and was gripping his throat, choking him. But Prosser's gloves were slippery with blood so he couldn't hold on well. At the same time, the terrorist was trying to bite Prosser's wrist, but instead he bit onto the face of Prosser's watch. (Prosser wears his watch with the face turned inward.) The terrorist had a mouthful of watch, but he somehow also managed to punch Prosser in the face.

When I shot the propane canister, Prosser had nearly strangled the guy, but my shots made Prosser think bad guys were coming, so he released the terrorist's throat and snatched out the pistol from his holster, just as SSG Konkol, Lewis, Devereaux, and Muse swarmed the shop. But the shots and the propane fiasco also had brought the terrorist back to life, so Prosser quickly reholstered his pistol and subdued him by smashing his face into the concrete.

The combat drama was ended, so I started snapping photos again.

When Recon Platoon showed up about a minute later, SFC Bowman asked LTC Kurilla to lie down. But Kurilla was ordering people to put out security and directing action this way and that. When the very experienced medic Specialist Munoz put morphine into Kurilla, the commander still kept giving orders, even telling Munoz how to do his job. So SFC Bowman told Munoz to give Kurilla another morphine, and finally Kurilla settled down, and stopped giving orders long enough for them to haul him and the terrorist away to the Combat Support Hospital.

★   ★   ★

There are times when the counterinsurgency simply is still too kinetic to spend much time baby-kissing. The Deuce Four was a warrior cult, with one mission: winning Mosul. And Kurilla was the cult leader. Iraqis respond very favorably to strong and just leadership. They respond very favorably to total hard-core soldiers, killers, who can take hits and keep on going, but who treat the people with justice and dignity.

After firefights, Kurilla made a practice of strolling around the markets and haggling over the price of sheep he'd buy as rewards for Iraqi soldiers or police who performed bravely. As I walked with him, totally exposed, I mostly thought, "We are going to die." I spent a lot of time hitting the dirt, diving out of the line of imagined fire. Kurilla spent a lot of time laughing at me as I got up, not dead, and brushed off the dust or garbage. We both knew he was setting conditions for victory, showing NO FEAR time after time after time. Kurilla was aware of the danger. But he understood that Iraqis needed a strong leader to rally their own courage and he provided one. Cults draw strength from the leader.

The cult leader portrays what the cult members aspire to, or wish to affiliate with. But the play needs an audience. In counterinsurgency there is a media battlefield that must be won. Erik Kurilla understood this. And he used the tools available to him, like me. By my fourth or fifth month in the war, I had learned that moving around from unit to unit led to a tired writer doing a dozen or two missions without writing a word. Communications were an incessant problem. But someone in the Deuce Four must have read Ernie Pyle's article about how the 9th Division became a media magnet in World War II simply by supplying a reporter with everything he needed, including a jeep and driver twenty-four hours a day. The Deuce Four gave me a trailer and an Internet line and all the missions I could handle and broke rules to help me. And they were great copy. So I stayed with them until they rotated home almost six months later. The cult gained a world-wide readership through my Web site.

Within my first days there, Kurilla said something to me like, "You'll have a Deuce Four tattoo before you leave here." I laughed that one off because I don't do tattoos for anything or anybody. By the time those five plus months ended, the Deuce Four was tattooed on my soul. Kurilla's command cult derived from his being a true warrior, but also from his understanding of the importance of presentation and respect for others, along with being smart enough to dial in the media, in an army that really doesn't like soldiers who are good at media.

The next day, Iraqi Army and police commanders were in a fury that LTC Kurilla had been shot. Some blamed his men, while others blamed the terrorists, although blame could not compete with disbelief. Kurilla had gone on missions every single day for almost a year: talking with people downtown; interfacing with shop owners; conferencing with doctors; drinking tea with Iraqi citizens in their homes; meeting proud mothers with new babies. It's important to interact and to take the pulse of a city in a war where there is no "behind the lines," no safe areas.

Soon after Kurilla got shot, over a meal in the dining facility with Chaplain Wilson and our two battalion surgeons, Major Brown and Captain Warr, there was much discussion about the "ethics" of war and contention about why we afford top-notch medical treatment to terrorists. (The terrorist that Prosser had turned into a eunuch lay in the same recovery area as Kurilla. Kurilla could see him from his bed.) The treatment terrorists get here is better and more expensive than what many Americans or Europeans can get.

★　　★　　★

"That's the *difference* between the terrorists and us," Chaplain Wilson kept saying. "Don't you understand? *That's* the difference."

For all his many great qualities—Kurilla must be one of the

finest weapons in the U.S. arsenal—nobody is good at everything. I think if Kurilla suddenly found himself governing a peaceful neighborhood in Baghdad, he might become a pain, like a lion suddenly forced to live on canned food.

Kurilla did not win all his media battles—some people found him abrasive. We argued in the early days, and I thought he was going to kick me out. But he and the Deuce Four mopped the floor with enemy blood *and* ink, creating conditions that allowed Iraqis and Americans to retake Mosul from the insurgents and criminals. It was a grand performance, and what happened after the Deuce Four and 1st Brigade of which they were a part rotated out, only proves the point.

When their deployment ended in the autumn of 2005, the approximately eight thousand soldiers of the Brigade were replaced by the 172nd Stryker Brigade Combat Team from Alaska, which at any given time had probably three to five thousand men in the area. (Some units had been detailed elsewhere.) Both units made enormous progress in securing the city compared to the chaos of December 2004, largely by focusing on recruiting, organizing, and training the Iraqi Police and Army.

When I got back to Mosul in January 2007, the city was held by a single battalion. So during the initial invasion, General David Petraeus's 101st Airborne Division took Nineveh province with more than twenty thousand soldiers, most of whom ended up in and around Mosul. By 2005, somewhat over eight thousand troops remained, to be replaced by somewhere between three to five thousand. In January 2007, there were only about seven hundred fifty soldiers of the 2nd Battalion of the 7th Cavalry (known as the 2-7 CAV), whose deployment to Mosul had just begun. This was possible only because the Iraqi Army, or parts of it, had made astounding progress in a couple of years.

And yet all of this progress was in the manner of two steps

backward and one step forward; the Mosul I returned to in early 2007 was a place whose future seemed far more in doubt than in mid-2003 when Petraeus was rapidly returning the city to normal life, except sans Saddam, which seemed to mean a better life.

CHAPTER FIVE

The Winter of Our Discontent

That first night back in Mosul in January 2007, Command Sergeant Major Jeff Mellinger, along with his handful of soldiers, and I drove out with the 2-7 CAV, commanded by Lieutenant Colonel Eric Welsh. The 2-7 CAV would end up doing some of the most outstanding work in Iraq I had seen.

That night, we drove over a gigantic bomb buried deep in the road. The bomb contained roughly fifteen hundred pounds of explosives and was big enough to obliterate a tank. Sometimes these "deep buried" IEDs are hidden for months before being detonated by the watching enemy. We drove right over it. But the enemy did not strike. Not that time.

With about seven hundred fifty soldiers, Welsh and the 2-7 could not secure Mosul themselves. They would eventually be fielding about four hundred actual war fighters onto the streets of Mosul with a population of about 1.7 million. Instead the 2-7's job was to leverage the two Iraqi divisions in the region, along with Iraqi Police, into an effective fighting force.

In essence, the 2-7 was acting like a giant Special Forces team. Special Forces perform various types of missions ranging from Direct Action or DA, as in a rapidly executed raid on a specific target, to Counterterrorism (CT) and Counterinsurgency (COIN) programs, for winning the political war for the trust of the populace—though 2-7 did not have enough troops to conduct true counterinsurgency.

Then there is FID, or Foreign Internal Defense, wherein our guys train and lead a foreign army or police force. In FID, typically a twelve-man "A-team" trains up and runs operations with a battalion-sized element. In Mosul the 2-7 did most of the things Special Forces do, but the overarching mission was FID, or at least FID-like. Small groups of 2-7 soldiers were running operations with much larger groups of Iraqi soldiers and police. The 2-7 was fighting hard and often. But the Iraqis were shouldering most of the daily burden, making this a classic Special Forces scenario, but on a much larger scale with 2-7 soldiers who were not versed in Special Forces doctrine. Nevertheless, they were adapting quickly, and the Iraqis were proving to be increasingly competent fighters.

That the 2-7 could function in this way was evidence both of the enormous progress of the Iraqi security forces in the region and of how much the 2-7's predecessors had done to quell the violence in Mosul. In late 2004, when the Deuce Four arrived in Mosul, the enemy was launching dozens of attacks every day, far more than in January 2007. But the 2-7 had less than one-tenth the Coalition force that was there in 2005, and only about one-thirtieth of the 2003 force. This was just one of the problems created by not having enough troops; when a place started to do better, troops were sucked out and squirted onto fires elsewhere, leaving behind, it seemed at times, barely enough to keep the base from being overrun. But this also was a sign of great progress. That a single battalion was not swallowed alive was strong evidence of growing momentum.

Progress but certainly not victory. Mosul had been stripped of troops not because it was safe but because Baghdad and its surrounds were collapsing into violence and chaos. Mosul was still broken.

Moreover, it was clear that the 2-7 was headed for a death match. The terrorists always went on the attack when a new unit took over. And although up in Mosul "the surge" was still a rumor, if the plan worked down south, odds were the fleeing terrorists would descend on the northern city again as they had in the fall of 2004 after Fallujah.

The Ghost Battalion

The 2-7 goes by the name of "The Ghost Battalion" for its legendary stand in the Korean War, where against impossible odds and enormous casualties, the cavalry still kept fighting. Units with a great history embrace the disasters as well as the victories, as long as the soldiers fought and died well. And there was also Custer, and the marching song, the "Garry Owen":

We are the pride of the Army,
And a regiment of great renown,
Our names on the pages of history,
From sixty-six on down.
If you think we stop or falter,
While into the fray we're goin'
Just watch the step with our heads erect
When our band plays 'Garry Owen.'

If the 2-7 walked in the shadow of its own legends, so did their commander. Orphaned at the age of nine, Eric Welsh grew up in a foster home knowing little about his biological parents. Then years later as an army infantry officer on assignment at the Pentagon, he accidentally picked up the scent of his family. A clue to an uncle he had never known fell into his lap. Welsh was a lieutenant colonel by the time he tracked down the retired Vietnam fighter pilot. The uncle was not particularly open to overtures, especially from strangers with dubious claims of familial ties. With good reason: for years the man had been fending off unsavory journalists posing as something else, none of whom were interested in him, except as a pathway to his legendary father.

But Welsh's uncle Greg really was the brother of Welsh's mother. And both his mother and his uncle were children of Pappy Boyington, Medal of Honor recipient, former POW, a man so renowned for his ferocity and courage that a famous television show was built around the Black Sheep Squadron he led during World War II. (*Baa, Baa Black Sheep*, starring Robert Conrad.) And so in January 2007 and for most of the next year, the fate of Mosul rested on the shoulders of Boyington's grandson and seven hundred fifty spiritual sons of General George Armstrong Custer.

For Lack of a Nail

The two Iraqi Army divisions operating in Nineveh at the time relied on the 2-7 CAV for logistical support. Meanwhile, the Coalition Force had decided to cut off the free fuel it had been supplying to the Iraqi Army. The Coalition wanted the Iraqis to learn to handle their own logistical solutions.

In Mosul the Iraqi Army's logistical solution was to scale back patrols to save gas. That meant roads that should have been swept for bombs persistently were ignored for days. I arrived for my embed with the 2-7 the first week of January 2007. On January

15, a 2-7 Humvee rolled down one of those under-patrolled roads, the road we drove that first night with CSM Mellinger.

There were five men in the Humvee: Second Lieutenant Mark Daily born in Irvine, California; Staff Sergeant John Cooper born in Cleveland, Ohio; Sergeant Ian Anderson born in Prairie Village, Kansas; and Specialist Matthew Grimm from Wisconsin Rapids, Wisconsin. Matt Grimm had recently been awarded a Purple Heart for injuries he'd suffered while driving another Humvee that was struck by a rocket-propelled grenade that killed another soldier. Matt was driving again on January 15. The fifth occupant, "Jacob," a Christian Assyrian-Iraqi, born in Mosul in 1967, was performing arguably the most dangerous job in Iraq: interpreter for American combat forces. The Kurdish interpreters for American forces were treated like rock stars and heroes in the Kurdish north; Kurdish kids would ask for their autographs. And with good reason. I cannot remember all the stories of Iraqi interpreters who were killed. And while the Kurdish kids wanted their autographs, al Qaeda wanted their heads. Many Arab interpreters, who could not reach the safety of the Kurdish north, were murdered. But out on the streets the bombs were for everyone.

Just next to the road were two occupied two-story houses and an unfinished house from which terrorists had run a wire to the explosive. As the Humvee was passing over the estimated fifteen hundred-pound bomb, the enemy detonated it. Pieces of the Humvee weighing hundreds of pounds flew as far as two hundred yards away, some crashing atop the second stories of Iraqi homes. All five men died within a fraction of a second, almost certainly never knowing what happened.

Back at FOB Marez, James Pippin, Command Sergeant Major of the 2-7, immediately prepared to roll out. I traveled with Pippin to the site of the blast, which had not yet been secured.

Pippin took charge of the scene—officers and enlisted men alike—and set the tone for the recovery, working first on security and finding his lost soldiers. Pippin wanted every piece of man and machine out of there, a respectful battlefield recovery and identification of remains.

The smell of fuel and wreckage had a chokehold on the debris-covered field. The damage was jaggedly inconsistent. Radios were shattered, but paper merely scattered. Night-vision devices were blown to pieces; MREs (packaged meals ready to eat) were tossed around but otherwise completely unharmed, not even scorched.

The families who lived in the two houses closest to the bomb claimed ignorance. A man from the first house was upset that debris had landed on his roof. After such attacks, Iraqis often get paid by the Americans for damages, so he could have been trying to establish a claim.

It seemed inconceivable that the enemy could remove perhaps fifteen hundred pounds of soil and replace it with 1, pounds of explosives without anyone in either house noticing something. I looked at the man on the roof who was complaining about the debris, and dark thoughts fell upon me.

In this counterinsurgency the most powerful weapon is a cell phone in the hands of a citizen who has decided the future belongs not to the terrorists but to the people killing the terrorists. But Welsh and seven hundred fifty men were in no position to wage a true counterinsurgency in the second largest city in Iraq. Petraeus with twenty thousand men, and at first no local insurgency to speak of, had far more "cops" to walk the beat and recruit neighbors to the cause of their own security. The Iraqi Army may have been short of gas, but in January 2007 we had the bigger problem. *We were short of troops and friends—or at least friends ready to stand up with us—or for themselves.*

But there are always some.

The Martyr

The murderer was dressed as a woman as he walked down the alley toward the mosque full of worshippers. It was Friday, late in January, just before the Muslim holy day of Ashura, and the air was chilled in the small village north of Mosul.

The bomb strapped to the murderer's body was studded with ball bearings so that he could kill many villagers as they gathered for prayer. The detonation would eviscerate and dismember those closest, shattering bones into fragments. The ball bearings would extend the killing beyond the percussive edge of the blast, ripping through the flesh of those who survived the shockwave.

There were no soldiers in his path to stop him, no police to alert. There were only the villagers and a mass murderer done up for a masquerade. In the mosque more than one hundred people were praying.

The prayerful people did not know he was coming, but we hear the explosions every day. I remember the story of another such man who had grabbed the hand of a nearby child as cover, then walked over to a policeman before detonating himself and the child. I remember the bomber who rammed a car full of explosives into a vehicle full of American soldiers surrounded by Iraqi children. The bomber could have waited a block or two and attacked the Americans man-on-man. He chose to blow up the children. Sometimes we see the torn and mangled hunks of flesh and watch the open bodies curl a baleful steam into the cold morning air.

As the murderer walked purposefully toward his target, there was a village man in his path. But under the guise of a simple villager this was a true martyr, and he, too, had his target in sight. The martyr had seen through the disguise. But he had no gun. No bomb. No rocket. No stone. No time.

The martyr walked up to the murderer and lunged into a bear hug.

The blast ripped the martyr to pieces mixing his flesh with the flesh of the murderer. Ball bearings shot through the alley and wounded two children, but the people in the mosque were saved. And the martyr's children, who surely had felt his arms around them many times, saw his love more than ever in his last embrace.

Home of the Roughnecks

Days after the bomb killed all five men in the Humvee, the Iraqis developed a positive ID on individuals suspected in that attack. American Green Berets had told me the Iraqi SWAT team in Mosul was very good. They were right. I watched their final preparations, including a rehearsal of the mission to kill or capture the suspects believed to be holed up in a house. The Iraqis would run the actual breach and entry, backed up by other American elements, including the 2-7 Cavalry. I was to accompany the mission.

The cold hours of the night ticked by until about 2:00 A.M., when Eric Welsh's Humvee rolled off base with me in the backseat. Various American military units crept around the target in other Humvees. Through the night-vision monocular attached to my helmet, I could make out flashes as the SWAT team used explosives to enter the house. Moments later I saw "flash-bang" grenades being used by the entry team to stun the occupants.

We moved in at about 3:19 A.M., after the Iraqis and other American forces had secured the place, having already found weapons, a small amount of explosives, and a computer inside the well-furnished, two-story home. Four men were detained. We couldn't have been in the house more than four minutes when a radio call to Welsh announced that the enemy was afoot nearby.

While we were launching the raid, about fifteen to twenty

enemy fighters had been assembling to launch a mortar attack against FOB Marez from which we had just come. As the SWAT team was penetrating the house, the enemy was attaching mortar tubes to base plates, adjusting the bipods, and dialing elevation and deflection—pulling the safety pins off the mortar fuses.

While most of our soldiers were asleep on base, the enemy crews began dropping mortars into the tubes. BAM! The first mortar bomb arced over Mosul, sailing over the rooftops, slicing through the dark, tracing a parabola toward its target.

Back at the American base, the Q36 counter-battery radar was on guard, sweeping the skies of Mosul with its invisible electro-magnetic wash. The beam was like a flashlight and the mortar bomb like a mirror against a dark sky. Blip. The Q36 caught a glint and registered the precise time and location. Blip. Blip. Blip. Photons tickled electrons; the computer registered data points and calculated the POO (Point of Origin) and POI (Point of Impact).

More bombs were fired into the dark sky: blipblipblipblip. They kept coming, arcing above Mosul, over the base perimeter, and past the guards. The mortar fins kept the noses pointed forward and then downward . . . down, down, down . . . BAM!!!! goes the bomb when it's close, and when farther: KARUMMPHH!!! But back with the Iraqi SWAT team at that well-furnished house, we were too far from the base to hear the explosions.

American technology is good at tracking the source of such an attack. From lethal experience the enemy knows they must be on the move within minutes—which sometimes still is not fast enough—so they shot only eight bombs. Unfortunately for the terrorists, the 2-7 was in Mosul on the raid. Now we were getting ready to welcome them home.

In the air, the "Roughneck" Scout Weapons Platoon (1-17 CAV from the 82nd Airborne) buzzed over Mosul supporting our raid, their little Kiowa helicopters armed with rockets and machine guns. We call the little helicopters "warriors"; the enemy calls them "mosquitoes."

Hovering above the mosquitoes, peering through the night into the Mosul warren, was the AirScan reconnaissance airplane, owned and piloted by civilians contracted by the American government. The enemy may have heard the aircraft, which captured video of them maneuvering, running, and dodging for overhead cover.

The Roughneck pilots flying their Kiowas left us behind and vrrrrooommmmed across the Tigris River toward the source of the mortars. Welsh rushed out of the house, and we ran to the Humvees, racing through the streets of Mosul. The enemy had apparently shown up with about the same number of people we had. Our advantage was two helicopters with limited ammunition. The enemy advantage was nearly everything else.

Ground contact was imminent. The Kiowas had gotten PID (positive identification) and fired rockets into the men. The enemy was somewhere close around us and probably heavily armed. Darkness wouldn't offer concealment much longer; if we got into a decisive fight, the sun would rise on us.

As we made our way into the warren, a helicopter swooped low and invisibly overhead with machine gun firing. I knew the pilots would not fire unless they had PID, and the helicopter flying so low over our Humvee while firing its machine gun meant the enemy was very close.

At about 3:51 A.M., a lone ambulance raced up a deserted street, its red lights flashing. Knowing the enemy used ambulances to smuggle terrorists away from fights, Welsh ordered his soldiers to stop it. The men inside claimed to be on a routine call. Welsh told his soldiers to release them and act like all was well, but to follow the ambulance, which they did. The two men inside the ambulance apparently did not notice the tail.

The ambulance headed down the road and stopped in a densely populated warren of narrow streets and alleys, lights still flashing. As we watched, some men emerged from an alley on the right where the ambulance waited, unaware that American troops had converged on the scene. About eight men booked toward the flashing lights of the ambulance. Two were wounded.

Welsh's simple plan had worked, but this was fantastically dangerous. Urban combat greatly favors the enemy. The far end of the alley reeked of sudden death. But that was where the men dashing for the ambulance had come from so that was where our guys were going.

I saw shades of black, green, and white through my night-vision monocular while my other eye was pulled to the red light of the ambulance throbbing off the wall. The soldiers checked for ambushes amid the shops and doorways all around us. The time was just after 4:00 A.M., and the cold in that alley was foul and wet. Every place is a bad place to get shot, but this was worse than most; infection from wounds sustained in places like this kills soldiers in Iraq.

Our soldiers detained the men who had run for the ambulance, searched, and flex-cuffed them. But the two wounded men were already in the ambulance, still parked on the road. Welsh decided to let them go. I couldn't shake the question from my head: Why did he let the wounded guys go?

As the ambulance drove away, our guys questioned the detainees. One man said that he had just woken up and gone outside for some reason. But A. J., the Kurdish interpreter, noticed the man was wearing socks. A. J. explained that most Iraqis won't sleep wearing socks, because folk wisdom says that sleeping with socks on can make one go blind. (I am not making that up.)

The soldiers kept their weapons trained on the little arch at the end of the alley. There might be more enemy back there. We could have used a few more guns for that alley. The Kiowas vvr-rrroooming overhead couldn't help; we were too close to the enemy. When it's tight like this, high-tech advantages vanish and it's man on man. And when the other man can dive out of a doorway and stab you in the throat, he can win without firing a shot and disappear into the warren where walls often have hidden passages. Even the night-vision monocular can be a liability this close, because it comes into and out of focus. Then if you flip up the monocular, that eye is useless because the device has completely disabled your normal night vision.

I felt for my latch-on medical kit where the tourniquet waited and felt for my knife to cut off rifle slings to make extras. My ears strained for any sound.

A soldier walked silently toward me, moving forward to help clear the alley. A sliver of green haloed his eye—his night-vision monocular. Deadly serious, he pulled out a pistol and said, "Here, sir," moving to hand it to me. "I can't take that," I said, "It's against the rules." He must have thought I was a complete idiot, but he reholstered the pistol and went ahead, rifle at the ready.

Time dragged. I kept thinking: Why had Welsh let those two guys in the ambulance go? Were the four detainees from the house raid the same ones who killed our guys some days earlier?

A soldier pulled out a piece of chalk and scrawled "U.S." with an arrow underneath pointing down the alley to make it easier to find where soldiers had gone, and there was just enough ambient light to read it. Clearing the alley, soldiers disappeared into the archway. Ordinarily, I would follow. But if there were close combat I would just be in the way, and ricochets in that tunnel would nearly guarantee that everyone in there would be hit. Some soldiers cleared, others kept watch. The detainees were given vapor trace tests, which found no indication of explosives, and then put into Humvees.

The time was 5:14 A.M. and the sun would soon rise over Mosul. LTC Welsh radioed to the Iraqi Army and asked them to send some men to the hospital where the ambulance was taking the two wounded guys. Playing dumb, the Iraqi soldiers offered the wounded guys transportation home. Once they got there, the Iraqi soldiers searched the home and found six dead men. No need for an autopsy; this was death by Roughnecks. The prisoners also told the Iraqi soldiers where to find the mortar tubes hidden down by the Tigris.

One battalion of Americans in the second or third largest city in Iraq. Welsh and his men were being tested by a tough and adaptable enemy who would avoid our superior firepower and try to whittle down the 2-7 with brief lightning attacks. But Welsh had his own plan: he was going on the attack and he was not going to let up. Fighting alongside the 2-7 would be the Iraqi Army and Police as terrorists fell back on the city, fleeing the offensive taking shape to the south. The peril of the situation was not lost on these soldier sons of General Custer.

CHAPTER SIX

Petraeus Takes Command

I was with some Iraqis in Mosul in January 2007 when word spread that Petraeus would be taking over as commanding general. One Iraqi said, "Petraeus will be in charge again, the war will end."

My own reaction was more cautious. But there was no doubt we were getting something that can be rare in this life: a second chance. This was no slight on General George Casey, who worked hard and made great progress, but he never had enough troops or enough time. Casey had admirable war-fighting skills; I could see that from the ground. But his media skills weren't as strong. Casey wasn't actually "bad" with the media like Lieutenant General Ricardo Sanchez, who could transmute wine into vinegar with a glance, yet Casey was not adept in the media battle space, and that hobbled him in a high-intensity counterinsurgency.

I thought General Petraeus could turn this war around not just because of the success he had in Mosul but because he had seen that success unravel. He knew how counterinsurgency could work and he knew what could make it fail.

The son of a Dutch ship captain who sailed a Liberty Ship during World War II, David Petraeus grew up in Cornwall-on-Hudson, New York, just a few miles from West Point, where he graduated near the top of his class in 1974, and married the daughter of the commandant.

In his doctoral dissertation, *The American Military and the Lessons of Vietnam: A Study of Military Influence and the Use of Force in the Post-Vietnam Era*, Petraeus deconstructed the myth of an American military leadership eager to rush into battle. Studying the history of American military involvement in the post-World War II era, particularly the civilian-military interface and decision-making process, he found that military leaders were often more cautious in the application of military force than presidents, their advisers, and civilian leaders in the Pentagon. Part of this caution was due, in his analysis, to the lessons of Vietnam, where the military leadership learned the limits of American military power. "In particular, Vietnam planted in the minds of many in the military doubts about the ability of U.S. forces to conduct successful large-scale counterinsurgencies."

As Petraeus wrote: "Vietnam was an extremely painful reminder that when it comes to intervention, time and patience are not American virtues in abundant supply."

The Vietnam experience had shaped a generation of military leaders, many of whom were skeptical about what Petraeus had accomplished in Mosul. They believed counterinsurgency would always take longer than average citizens realize or politicians will admit. Petraeus's dissertation showed he went into Iraq with eyes wide open—he knew how difficult it was to fight a counterinsurgency. That he went in and did it anyway reveals much about the man.

Second Chances

During a mission one day that took us from Baqubah to Baghdad, Lieutenant Colonel Fred Johnson told me a story about General Petraeus. Back when Johnson was a captain, and Petraeus was a colonel, Petraeus was Johnson's new commander. They were conducting a live-fire exercise when a young soldier named Specialist Terrence Jones tripped and accidentally fired his weapon. Jones shot Colonel Petraeus, the bullet slamming through his chest and taking a piece of his back on the way out. Petraeus fell to the ground, bleeding out of his mouth. He nearly died. We nearly lost the man who may prove to be the most important military leader in a generation.

The army is not forgiving of such incidents. The best that Captain Johnson and Specialist Jones could reasonably have hoped for was a painless end to their military service. Johnson looked me in the eye and said, "You know what Petraeus did?"

"What?" I asked.

"He gave me a second chance."

Fred Johnson actually got picked up for promotion early.

"What happened to the soldier?" I asked, thinking surely there had to be a consequence. Conventional wisdom holds that a soldier just can't shoot a commander in the chest and walk away unpunished. There is no such thing as an "accidental discharge." Unplanned bullet launches are called "negligent discharges." As in negligent homicide.

"Mike, you won't believe how Jones was punished," Johnson said. "Petraeus sent him to ranger school."

I couldn't believe my ears. That's a punishment a lot of young soldiers dream about. And that might explain why LTC Johnson sometimes says, "I believe in second chances," and "when someone gives you a second chance, you should pass it along."

Shortly after taking command in 2007, Petraeus wrote a letter to all the soldiers in the command. The subject was Values.

From General Petraeus:

Soldiers, Sailors, Airmen, Marines, and Coast Guardsmen serving in Multi-National Force-Iraq:

Our values and the laws governing warfare teach us to respect human dignity, maintain our integrity, and do what is right. Adherence to our values distinguishes us from our enemy. This fight depends on securing the population, which must understand that we—not our enemies—occupy the moral high ground. This strategy has shown results in recent months. Al Qaeda's indiscriminate attacks, for example, have finally started to turn a substantial proportion of the Iraqi population against it.

In view of this, I was concerned by the results of a recently released survey conducted last fall in Iraq that revealed an apparent unwillingness on the part of some U.S. personnel to report illegal actions taken by fellow members of their units. The study also indicated that a small percentage of those surveyed may have mistreated noncombatants. This survey should spur reflection on our conduct in combat.

I fully appreciate the emotions that one experiences in Iraq. I also know first hand the bonds between members of 'the brotherhood of the close fight.' Seeing a fellow trooper killed by a barbaric enemy can spark frustration, anger, and a desire for immediate revenge. As hard as it might be, however, we must not let these emotions lead us—or our comrades in arms—to commit hasty, illegal actions. In the event that we witness or hear of such actions, we must not let our bonds prevent us from speaking up.

Some may argue that we would be more effective if

we sanctioned torture or other expedient methods to obtain information from the enemy. They would be wrong. Beyond the basic fact that such actions are illegal, history shows that they also are frequently neither useful nor necessary. Certainly, extreme physical action can make someone 'talk;' however, what the individual says may be of questionable value. In fact, our experience in applying the interrogation standards laid out in the Army Field Manual (2-22.3) on Human Intelligence Collector Operations that was published last year shows that the techniques in the manual work effectively and humanely in eliciting information from detainees.

We are, indeed, warriors. We train to kill our enemies. We are engaged in combat, we must pursue the enemy relentlessly, and we must be violent at times. What sets us apart from our enemies in this fight, however, is how we behave. In everything we do, we must observe the standards and values that dictate that we treat noncombatants and detainees with dignity and respect. While we are warriors, we are also all human beings. Stress caused by lengthy deployments and combat is not a sign of weakness; it is a sign that we are human. If you feel such stress, do not hesitate to talk to your chain of command, your chaplain, or a medical expert.

We should use the survey results to renew our commitment to the values and standards that make us who we are and to spur re-examination of these issues. Leaders, in particular, need to discuss these issues with their troopers—and, as always, they need to set the right example and strive to ensure proper conduct. We should never underestimate the importance of good leadership and the difference it can make.

Thanks for what you continue to do. It is an honor to serve with each of you.

David H. Petraeus,

General, United States Army

Commanding

Interestingly, when I published the Values letter from General Petraeus, a large number of readers disparaged the general for taking such a position, as if it were something new and wrong, or even weak-minded. Maybe they were unaware that our own country was founded through insurgency against the British, and that our forefathers were intimately familiar with the application of insurgency and counterinsurgency. Maybe they were unaware of other generals in our lineage, such as General George Washington, who in a famous letter to Benedict Arnold, as Arnold was about to invade Canada in an attempt to persuade Canadians to join the U.S. in rebellion, laid down the classic principles of political war:

To COLONEL BENEDICT ARNOLD

Camp at Cambridge, September 14, 1775

Sir: You are intrusted with a Command of the utmost Consequence to the Interest and Liberties of America. Upon your Conduct and Courage and that of the Officers and Soldiers detached on this Expedition, not only the Success of the present Enterprize, and your own Honour, but the Safety and Welfare of the Whole Continent may depend. I charge you, therefore, and the Officers and Soldiers, under your Command, as you value your own Safety and Honour and the Favour and Esteem of your Country, that you consider yourselves, as marching, not through an Enemy's Country; but that of our Friends and Brethren, for such the Inhabitants of Canada, and the Indian Nations have approved themselves in this unhappy Contest between Great Britain and America. That you check by every Motive of Duty and Fear of Punishment, every Attempt to plunder or insult any of the Inhabitants of Canada. Should any American Soldier be so base and infamous as to injure any Canadian or Indian, in his Person or Property, I do most earnestly enjoin you to bring him to such severe and exemplary Punishment as the Enormity of the Crime may require. Should it extend to Death itself it will not be disproportional to its Guilt at such a Time and in such a Cause: But I hope and trust, that the brave Men who have voluntarily engaged in this Expedition, will be governed by far different Views, that Order, Discipline and Regularity of Behaviour will be as conspicuous, as their Courage and Valour. I also give it in Charge to you to avoid all Disrespect to or Contempt of the Religion of the Country and its Ceremonies. Prudence, Policy, and a true Christian Spirit, will lead us to look with Compassion upon their Errors without insulting them. While we are contending for our own Liberty, we should be very cautious of violating the Rights of Conscience in others, ever considering that God alone is the Judge of the Hearts of Men, and to him only in this Case, they are answerable. Upon the whole, Sir, I beg you to inculcate upon the Officers and Soldiers, the Necessity of preserving the strictest Order during their March through Canada; to represent to them the Shame, Disgrace, and Ruin to themselves and Country, if they should by their Conduct, turn the Hearts of our Brethren in Canada against us. And on the other Hand, the Honours and Rewards which await them, if by their Prudence and good Behaviour, they conciliate the Affections of the Canadians and Indians, to the great Interests of America, and convert those favorable Dispositions they have shewn into a lasting Union and Affection. Thus wishing you and the Officers and Soldiers under your Command, all Honour, Safety, and Success, I remain Sir, etc.

In another missive to Arnold on the same date, Washington elaborates on several points, reminding Arnold especially of the prime directive of political war, that the success of the operations "depends wholly upon the Spirit with which it is pushed, and the favorable Disposition of the Canadians and Indians." For that reason Arnold must consult and communicate with them "to discover the real Sentiments of the Canadians towards our Cause, and particularly as to this Expedition . . . ever bearing in Mind, that if they are averse to it and will not co-operate . . . it must fail" and therefore should not even be attempted. Washington urged Arnold to make every effort to demonstrate that the Americans were not coming "as Robbers or to make War upon them; but as the Friends and Supporters of their Liberties, as well as ours." Crucially soldiers and officers must realize that their own "Safety depends upon the Treatment of these People."

Theft and plunder even against enemies is forbidden not least because "it will create dreadful Apprehensions in our Friends, and when it is once begun, none can tell where it will stop." And here's one that should have been required reading at Abu Ghraib: Prisoners are to be treated with "Humanity and [K]indness" as all "Acts of Cruelty and Insult" will disgrace the American Arms, and irritate our Fellow Subjects against us."

How is it, that the United States, borne of insurgency begat by injustice, would so misunderstand it today?

There had been reports of prisoner abuse in Nineveh while Petraeus was in command. He handled the problem the way Abu

Ghraib should have been handled. One of his officers reported that prisoners might have been beaten. Petraeus ordered an internal investigation resulting in immediate action. Instead of covering up the abuse, he invited the Red Crescent to view conditions at his prison. He held a meeting with local leaders, where he told them that, yes, some unfortunate acts had occurred, but the situation had been fixed internally. We have made mistakes, the general acknowledged, but that's not the way we do business and it's not going to happen again.

Some think all of this talk of values is a sign of weakness. But in a counterinsurgency our greatest resource is not the overwhelming firepower we can bring to bear upon the enemy, or the high technology we can use to locate and identify him. Our most powerful weapon is our values.

And so more than two centuries ago, one of our greatest generals and our first president seemed to know all we needed to know about insurgency and counterinsurgency. Maybe General Washington understood it so well, because he had the heart of an insurgent and a statesman. But we had not strictly adhered to these values, and the war turned bad for us in Canada.

About two centuries later, we abandoned moral high ground in Vietnam and then in Iraq. Yet in 2007, we were getting a chance to win it back, making me wonder if we had a second chance to win back the media battle space too. When Petraeus returned to Iraq, the number of embedded journalists in the country increased from fewer than ten to more than fifty. I was still bogged down in Baghdad fighting with some Public Affairs Officers. I thought of an e-mail exchange with Petraeus shortly before he took command.

"Mike, are you coming back to Iraq?"

I replied:

"Sir, I'm in Mosul."

Now months later, exasperated, I sent him another e-mail, which began as follows:

"If our combat forces fought the way we fight the media war, we would all be dead."

And he fixed it immediately. Just like that. Because he knows how to win this kind of war.

CHAPTER SEVEN

De Oppresso Liber

The goal of every counterinsurgency is to make the people safe and secure from their oppressors and to help them stay safe and secure by learning to stand up for themselves. To help them help themselves, it is necessary to win their trust. It is necessary to deserve their trust.

In the U.S. military, counterinsurgency is the particular expertise of the Special Forces, whose official motto is *De Oppresso Liber*—to liberate the oppressed. But pulling off a successful counterinsurgency in a theater as large as Iraq, complicated by decades of dictatorship and sectarian animosities, requires shifting the entire fighting force into Special Forces mode.

In conventional combat, holding the high ground yields tactical advantage. In an insurgency, the decisive terrain is moral. The superior fighting force occupying the moral high ground holds a commanding position.

In conventional warfare, the ranks need to be tactically efficient; strategy is for generals. In a counterinsurgency we speak of "strategic corporals." The men in the ranks who interact with the populace will largely determine the outcome of the war. It takes only a few bad actors to ruin a lot of hard work. See Abu Ghraib.

In a counterinsurgency soldiers trained to kill find themselves in a Baghdad neighborhood talking with locals about sewage removal. Counterinsurgency is political war. Governments that can't remove sewage lose the people.

Though Vietnam convinced the U.S. military that Americans were not suited for counterinsurgency, the opposite is closer to the truth. Americans are naturally good at counterinsurgency. One might almost say we are good at counterinsurgency, because we are good at removing sewage. We see problems as challenges rather than insurmountable obstacles. It never occurs to us to think the sewage can't be removed, or to wait around for someone else to do it. To Iraqis this ready American assumption that problems can and will be solved at first seems naïve. But for that very reason, when we deliver we may shatter ancient prejudices and inspire new visions of possibility.

Part of counterinsurgency is soldiers letting themselves be Americans in the most romantic sense of the word. The American soldier is the most dangerous man in the world, and the Iraqis had to learn that before they would trust or respect us. But it was when they understood that these great-hearted warriors, who so enjoyed killing the enemy, are even happier helping to build a school or to make a neighborhood safe that we really got their attention.

I have called al Qaeda a cult, and so it is. But in another frame it is a gang—in many cities it has recruited young gang members to be its foot soldiers. And it models a gang notion of masculinity in which the cruelest, most destructive, and bullying are seen as the toughest and thus the most admired. What the American soldier at his best brings to counterinsurgency—by culture, by training, by long and honored tradition—is a different model in which the strongest—and most to be feared—is the one who protects and serves, who makes the people safe by putting himself at risk.

Insurgents need the people like fish need the water, as Mao may actually have said. The challenge of counterinsurgency is to discover why the people are protecting the insurgents and offer a better deal.

Of course, there are always some people you just have to kill. And some of the locals will be on your side from the beginning— you try to keep them alive. The vast majority will be somewhere in the middle. They're the swing vote. For four years we had been losing the swing vote. To get it back we would have to do what the guerrillas do: live among the people.

Petraeus's new strategy would put our soldiers out among the people. That would mean taking greater risks. Petraeus knew that. But, he would explain, we were fighting for the people's trust. To win that fight we would have to take risks and sometimes that would mean losing troops. If the strategy worked, casualties would decrease once areas were secured and held. But if we could not deprive the enemy of habitat in the neighborhoods our second chance would be lost. There would not be another.

On March 25, 2007, I took a Blackhawk helicopter to Forward Operating Base (FOB) Falcon in Baghdad, where the 1-4 Cavalry from Fort Riley, Kansas, had just begun a long tour. The battalion commander, LTC James Crider, along with his staff, gave a detailed briefing of their Area of Operations (AO). The 1-4 had been deployed in one of the most dangerous and lawless areas of the country. Their job was to make it safe, not for themselves, but for the people who lived there, or had lived there, and we hoped would come back. Exactly because Baghdad has always been an ethnically and religiously mixed city, the civil war and the ethnic cleansing that came with it had left entire neighborhoods nearly abandoned save for the rats, mongrel dogs picking through garbage, and wary semi-feral cats. Many al Qaeda had moved into the abandoned homes.

The 1-4 CAV were to be cops on the beat in a neighborhood that in early 2007 made the South Bronx look like a gated community. They'd just gotten to Baghdad, and in the last week or so they'd been hit by four IEDs. They had been lucky; no KIAs (Killed in Action) so far. All of LTC Crider's subordinate commanders were combat veterans, although many of the younger soldiers were just out of initial training.

An important element in Petraeus's strategy to get our soldiers out into the neighborhoods was to vastly increase the numbers of "Combat Outposts," or COPs. Like the storefront mini-stations used by a "community policing" strategy in high-crime neighborhoods, the COPs are intended to be accessible neighborhood institutions in the way a traditional military operating base—or a barricaded police precinct house-never could.

LTC Crider explained that COPs were to be established in nearly eighty Baghdad neighborhoods and staffed with a combination of American soldiers and Iraqi Army or Iraqi Police. The goal of each COP is to secure and stabilize a neighborhood and deprive terrorists of habitat by involving the community in its own security. The 1-4 was setting up COPs.

The 1-4 Area of Operations at that time butted up against the west side of the Tigris in Baghdad. The neighborhoods are, or were, mostly Sunni and Shia, predominantly Shia, with a couple of Catholic enclaves. The market in one of the larger Shia neighborhoods was open and vibrant. The Sunni areas were lacking some basic goods like propane gas for cooking. (Shia were said to be taking it.) Counterinsurgency means resolving reasons for discontent. The 1-4 began propane distribution.

The Shia areas are mostly quiet, but there is a large Jaysh al-Mahdi (JAM) presence. (JAM is a catch-all term describing various

Shia militias claiming some allegiance to Moqtada al Sadr—a nut-case—who at that time had apparently run away and was hiding again in Iran.)

LTC Crider explains that Iraqi-on-Iraqi crime is high. The 1-4 had found fourteen bodies in a week. Some were executed with their hands bound. One man appeared to be in his seventies.

After the briefing with LTC Crider, we had dinner in the dining facility, which had recently been hit by a rocket. The soldiers called it pure luck, but I was thinking some good shooting could have been involved. As we finished dinner, CNN was broadcasting a press conference from Baghdad with Iraqi Prime Minister Nouri al-Maliki and the UN Secretary General Ban Ki-moon. Just as Maliki finished saying that Baghdad was getting safer, a rocket struck about fifty meters away from him. A coup for the enemy, except that Maliki stood resolute while others, including the secretary general, ducked in fear. But the shot did buttress the good-shooting theory, not to mention underscoring the enemy's penchant for its own sort of impromptu press conferences.

The empty streets around Baghdad were witness to the devastation of years of rampant crime, civil war, and the sundry insurgencies. Yet even on those empty streets it was possible to pick out slivers of hope among the shards of glass.

In one neighborhood where residents had been subject to a methodical slaughter, our people found an abandoned Christian college bearing a name suggestive of all things Iraq: the Pontifical Babel College. Over the next few days, the 1-4 Cavalry would transform the Pontifical Babel College into "COP Amanche" (Apache + Comanche).

We stood outside the college while EOD (Explosive Ordnance Disposal) bomb experts and a bomb dog checked for ambush or explosives. Outside soldiers secured a wide perimeter: the enemy has been known to rig entire buildings as bombs.

Inside the place was surreal. It was a Catholic seminary. The owners had completely vacated. The last page that had been turned on one calendar was July 2006. But here we found pristine offices with brand new computers, printers, fax machines, and a giant copier. There was a well-kept library with books in various languages including Arabic, English, German, and French. There were classrooms and an auditorium with a stage. We could have been anywhere in America or Europe. Surrounded by chaos, explosions, and gunfire, abandoned for almost a year, the seminary had been spared even from looting. Jets flew overhead, while helicopters traversed the airspace, yet the only invader here was the thick layer of dust.

It was as if the inhabitants had been beamed up without warning. In reality they had left after getting death threats from men who make good on such threats every day in this city. But that did not explain why, in a land where looters steal screws and rip copper wire from walls, this college was left untouched. The power of prayer?

LTC Crider took special care that all the fine books were well cared for, that the computers and other valuables were inventoried and sealed into the library. Then he asked some Iraqis to help him find a priest or other church official to inspect the building and its property.

Intelligence had come in on that first night. The 1-4 headed off for a raid to get some men who were said to be murdering people. Soon we were running through the early morning streets of a densely packed Shia neighborhood. A voice started crying over a loudspeaker—"*ALLLLAAAAHHHHHH. . . .*" After running for about fifteen minutes, we made it to the target house. I was sweating under my body armor and helmet. Birds were singing before the morning dawn. Our soldiers moved to the entrance. A soldier pried open the gate and went in.

The raid provided plenty of exercise but, thankfully, no

killing. We returned to the college after sunrise. Except for soldiers who were pulling security, the men were sprawled all over. Combat soldiers can sleep anywhere—even curled on steps, with bricks as pillows.

When we came back into the library, a soldier was standing on a ladder. A company commander asked, "What are you doing?"

"Looking for something to read, sir."

"Nope. This doesn't belong to us. Get down from there and leave the books alone."

"Yes sir," the young soldier said, and he crawled down from the ladder.

With each new day, the 1-4 tightened up security in and around the Babel College. Living conditions improved quickly. At first we slept on mats in the hallways. Soon we got cots.

Would this COP work? A first test came as a group of soldiers set out to meet their neighbors.

Most of the families in the vicinity have fled. People are murdered nearby every day. The Iraqi Police and our soldiers told me that murders were down since the launch of the new security plan. Yet our people found fourteen human bodies in one week. The enemy kills entire families, including small children. March 2007 was one of the worst in the war for Iraqis, and the following three months would be the worst for the Coalition. Sometimes the darkest hour does come before the dawn.

Even on that very first day, when our soldiers had barely begun turning the seminary into COP Amanche 1-4, soldiers started handing out tip-line cards to locals. Meanwhile, I watched the kids for clues to what their parents thought about us. A few minutes from the COP, Iraqi families were waiting outside their homes for a chance to talk with soldiers. The men were happy to see us, but skeptical about our claims that we were going to stay. American soldiers have come there before, they say, but they never stayed. As soon as the Americans leave, the terrorists move back in. That leaves the locals in the middle of what amounts to a gang war, and we are one of the gangs.

LTC Crider assured the people that this time the Americans will stay until the Iraqis can take over. But many Iraqis seem to understand that the real decision makers are Americans at home. Still it's heartening that most of the Iraqis are not fearful of Americans. What many really want—and they tell me clearly when they see a camera—is to communicate directly with Americans at home.

The neighborhood was mostly Christian, but we visited a Sunni family living close to the COP. The father was happy to see the Americans move in. His next-door neighbors, a Shia family who'd left because of the violence, had moved back in the day after the COP opened.

We continued to walk around the neighborhood and to talk with other locals, including a couple of Christian families. One man had closed his shop after two close friends had been murdered there recently.

There was no electricity anywhere and garbage everywhere. Uncollected garbage is a "broken window" in community policing parlance, a symbol of chaos and lawlessness. Cleaning up our own area around the COP was one way to communicate our intention to stay. But our people also contracted with locals to pick up the garbage for the neighborhood. Soldiers built a small garbage-collection point. When the locals saw that the garbage truly was getting hauled away in trucks, they began using it immediately. Terrorists don't pick up the trash on the way back from blowing up electrical stations and murdering kids. Just a little trash hauling was bringing tentative smiles to Iraqis who probably had not smiled in a long, long time.

One day, driving down the road, we saw what appeared to be

a human corpse. Looking for bombs and snipers, some 1-4 troops stopped to check it out. Then I heard one of the commanders on the radio crack, "This one's not dead yet." Neither is Monty Python apparently.

Our medic, sitting beside me in the Humvee, went to check out the man. Soon he was standing, though shaky on his feet. He told the interpreter he had had a seizure and was out of medicine. He drank some water. Slowly he seemed to come around.

If COP Amanche's first days were any indicator, some day we might be saying the same thing about the neighborhood.

That was in March 2007. In September 2007, I received an update from LTC Crider that he had sent out to the Family and Friends of the 1-4 CAV. He gave me permission to publish it, and the complete letter, including LTC Crider's moving tribute to three soldiers of the 1-4 who had recently been killed in action, can be found at my website at http://www.michaelyon-online.com/wp/achievements-of-the-human-heart.htm. Much of the letter, which I quote here, focuses on the blossoming of the neighborhood in just the five months since I had been there.

September 07
Family and Friends of 1-4 CAV,

War is a very personal endeavor. We find ourselves here involved in close friendships with one another as well as with the many Iraqis we interact with every day on the streets. We are also very close to our interpreters who share every danger with us. . . .

Recently, I found myself in the 28th Combat Support Hospital emergency room where one of our most loyal interpreters was being treated after being injured in an attack. While his prognosis was excellent, he was very shaken. . . . Not knowing his own condition he told me he loved Americans and America. He made me promise that I would take his heart to America if he died. He was going to be fine (he left the hospital the next day), but I could not convince him, so I promised. . . .

While conditions in our area of responsibility are vastly improved from about four months ago, it remains a dangerous place. Since my last update, we have lost three of our best. . . .

The personal relationships built by the Troopers of 1-4 CAV with individuals on the streets here is the key. Like any good relationship, we care for the people in our area without condition. We are there every hour of every day and do our best to change the conditions on the ground that allow an insurgency to flourish. We will never detain or kill them all, so we work to create an environment where they cannot survive.

One other example, recently we had seven IEDs discovered or detonated in a single seven-day span. On every one, we got a phone call from a local national telling us exactly where it was, or we were called immediately after and told who emplaced it. For the record, not one IED was effective. . . .

While the situation is always fragile, we have the initiative and the enemy here spends much more time reacting to us than we do to him. He can hide from us but he cannot hide from his neighbor.

Once abandoned streets are now filled with families and budding entrepreneurs who continue to open new small businesses every week. We have made available grants for small businesses in our area, and they have become immensely popular as you can imagine. I cannot walk the streets without children asking me for a soccer ball and "chocolate" (meaning any kind of candy) and adults asking for a micro grant application or for the status of the one they already filled out. They use these grants to open new businesses or improve their existing one and it is working well.

Our area now has a men's fashion store, fish markets, pharmacies, bakeries, and even two new gyms. We recently helped refurbish a once neglected clinic into a first-class location for health care. They have a small lab, dentists, a sonogram machine, x-ray machine, and other new equipment. Our medical platoon recently spent several hours with local doctors and nurses treating patients for everyday aches and pains with donated medical supplies from a humanitarian organization. I even watched our physician's assistant pull a watermelon seed out of a young girl's ear (sound familiar to any one?).

We also recently completed work on a soccer field that is used nightly by the young people here. Much to our surprise, on the opening night, each team had '1-4 CAV' printed on the back of their soccer jerseys. It is not uncommon for us to see guys with these jerseys on walking down the street. A second soccer field will open shortly.

Next we are working to repair transformer and power line issues, open a private doctor's office, and recruit locals to serve in the Iraqi Police. There is always plenty to do.

. . . 1-4 CAV has the highest re-enlistment rate of any battalion level unit in all of Baghdad and A Troop has the highest re-enlistment rate of any company-level organization in all of Baghdad for this fiscal year. I don't know how many companies are in Baghdad right now, but there are a lot!

Each year, units are given a re-enlistment mission. . . . [T]he Squadron had a mission to re-enlist two soldiers who are still on their initial enlistment during this fiscal year. Well, we re-enlisted forty-two.

While each soldier re-enlists for their own personal reasons, I think it is safe to say that these soldiers believe in what they are doing, they see a difference because of their efforts, and they have tremendous NCO leadership. Who wouldn't want to be a part of that?

Prepared and loyal!

Duty First!

LTC Jim Crider

PHOTO SECTION

GATES OF FIRE: MOSUL 2005

In 2005, I spent nearly five months in Mosul covering the 1-24 Infantry Regiment, the "Deuce Four" under the Command of Lieutenant Colonel Erik Kurilla. The Deuce Four fought hard for a year taking nearly 25 percent casualties. On August 18, 2005, just as the Deuce Four's deployment was about to end, LTC Kurilla became the 181st and last casualty.

That morning, Sergeant Daniel Lama had been shot while on operations around Yarmook Traffic Circle in downtown Mosul. After calling SGT Lama's mother to tell her Daniel was OK, Kurilla led men of the Deuce Four out to find the shooters. I rode in Kurilla's Stryker.

Hearing reports of automatic weapons fire back at Yarmook Circle, we headed in that direction when LTC Kurilla spotted three men in a black Opal. Kurilla's his sixth sense kicked in. The chase was on, aided by a Kiowa Warrior helicopter.

One of the two Kiowa pilots leaned out with an M4 rifle and fired on the Opal. The armed men abandoned the car and fled on foot. About 15 seconds later our ramp dropped. We ran into combat. Urban combat.

There were shops, alleys, doorways, windows.

Shots were fired behind us, but around a corner to the left. LTC Kurilla began running in the direction of the shooting. He passed by me and I chased, Kurilla leading the way.

There was a quick and heavy volume of fire. And then LTC Kurilla was shot.

Kurilla was running while he was hit in three places including his femur, which was shattered. The commander didn't seem to miss a stride. He did a crazy judo roll and came up shooting.

BamBamBamBam! Bullets were hitting all around Kurilla.

LTC Kurilla (front right) the moment the bullets strike.

Three bullets reach flesh. One snaps his thigh bone in half.

The young second lieutenant and specialist who were part of Kurilla's crew that day were the only two soldiers nearby. Neither had real combat experience. "A. H." (the interpreter) had no weapon. I had a camera.

**The commander rolls into a firing position just as
a bullet strikes the wall beside the 2LT's head.**

Kurilla, though down and unable to move, was fighting and firing, yelling at the two young soldiers to get in there, but they hesitated. BamBamBamBam!

The commander fights . . .

. . . and fights.

I screamed to the young soldiers, "Throw a grenade in there!" but they were not attacking. They didn't have grenades . . . or the combat experience to grasp the power of momentum.

Help arrived in the form of one man: Command Sergeant Major Prosser. Prosser ran around the corner, passed the two young soldiers, who were crouched low, and me, and started firing at a man inside who was trying to shoot Kurilla with a pistol.

Prosser shot the man at least four times with his M4 rifle. But the American M4 rifles are weak. The man just staggered back, regrouped, and tried to shoot Prosser. Then Prosser's M4 went "black" (no more bullets). Prosser threw down his empty M4, ran into the shop, and tackled the man.

I saw the very bloody leg of CSM Prosser inside the shop. He appeared to be shot down and dead. I saw Prosser's M4 on the ground.

CSM Robert Prosser "goes black."

I picked up Prosser's M4. "Give me some ammo! Give me a magazine!" I yelled, and the young 2LT handed over a full 30-round magazine.

I ran back to the corner of the shop and looked at LTC Kurilla who was bleeding, then saw CSM Prosser's extremely bloody leg inside the shop; the rest of Prosser was still obscured from view. I was going to run into the shop and shoot every man with a gun. And I was scared to death.

Reaching around the corner, I fired three shots into the dark shop. The third bullet pierced a propane canister which took off straight for my head but missed.

Luckily four soldiers from Alpha Company had arrived on the scene and LTC Kurilla directed them into the shop to help CSM Prosser.

Prosser wasn't dead, he was fighting hand-to-hand, while the

CSM Prosser, his leg drenched in the terrorist's blood, as Alpha Company 2nd Platoon arrives.

CSM Prosser drags the terrorist into the light.

terrorist was trying to bite Prosser's wrist, but instead he bit onto the face of Prosser's watch. Prosser subdued him by smashing his face into the concrete.

The combat drama was ended, so I started snapping photos again.

When Recon Platoon showed up about a minute later, Kurilla

LTC Kurilla being treated. He not only recovered but, as this book goes to press, is on his way back to Iraq for his fourth combat tour.

Prosser stands above the crocodile who bit his watch.

finally stopped giving orders long enough for medics to haul him and the terrorist away to the Combat Support Hospital, where Sergeant Lama was recovering.

SGT Daniel Lama recovering.

'Look What Al Qaeda Has Done to My Country'

In the closing days of June 2007, soldiers from Charley Company 1-12 CAV and Iraqi soldiers from the 5th IA, closed in on al Ahamir, a village on the outskirts of Baqubah that had been seized by al Qaeda. Al Ahamir's location—on the main road, about 3.5 miles from FOB Warhorse—made it an ideal place for attacking Americans and Iraqis. The soldiers approached cautiously, anticipating a typical enemy tactic: a village wired end to end with bombs and booby traps. One by one, experts destroyed the bombs that riddled the grounds, as they slowly progressed into the village, engaging in a small firefight.

They found more than bombs.

I came to al Ahamir the next morning. As we passed through the village, Captain Combs pointed out the nice houses, saying the people had been simple farmers with comfortable homes and lives. Until al Qaeda came.

The houses were empty. We passed by two donkeys each shot in the neck. Booby-trapping animal—or human—corpses is a favorite al Qaeda trick, so we are careful.

Al Qaeda had killed their livestock and all the people were gone. But where?

A short walk later, as we passed more abandoned homes, I saw an empty AK-47 magazine on the ground. The houses were in shambles: broken glass and ski masks littered the area. The Iraqi soldier with the goggles saw a photograph on the ground and picked it up.

We continued back into thick undergrowth just outside the village. The air temperature was about 115F. A terrible stench came from some palm groves. Soldiers from the 5th IA said they'd found some of the villagers: They were dead, stashed in shallow graves. Some of the bodies were fresh.

I told the Iraqi commander, Captain Baker, that it was important that Americans see this; he took me around the graves and showed more than I wanted to see. He said the people had been murdered by al Qaeda. I made video of him speaking and of the horrible scene. The heat and stench were oppressive and broken only by the sounds of shovels as Iraqi soldiers kept digging.

Baker was an impressive soldier, trained by American Special Forces. During the battle of Fallujah, Baker's men stayed and fought alongside American forces.

By the time I arrived, the Iraqi Scorpion Company soldiers had uncovered parts of six bodies. The people did not all appear to have been murdered at once. In one grave, there were exposed ribs and other bones, although there was still flesh on the bones.

The digging was the first part of the gruesome job. It was hot, hard work. As it progressed, the stench got worse and worse. An Iraqi soldier carefully sprinkled water on the corpses.

The Iraqi soldiers were barely talking. All had grim looks on their faces and everybody seemed to want to be a million miles away.

Iraqi soldiers said that al Qaeda had cut the heads off the children. One of the heads still had hair.

Had al Qaeda murdered the children in front of their parents? It could have been the other way around—they might have murdered the parents in front of the children. Or maybe they had

forced fathers to dig the graves of their children. A Baqubah city official later told me that he believes hundreds of people were murdered and buried in this immediate area.

I turned the video camera on Baker and asked him what he wanted to say to Americans. Through his interpreter, Baker said, "I want to tell the people of the United States, 'look what al Qaeda has done to my country. This is al Qaeda crimes, in our villages, in our homes. They killed the children. They kill anyone—Sunni, Shia, Kurdi—they don't care about religion or sect. I dug these bodies with my hands, this is not a fabrication, this is al Qaeda in Iraq and the horrible crimes they commit against Iraqi people.'"

Captain Baker

COME HOME

Come home, come home, You who are weary, come home.
WILL L. THOMPSON, "SOFTLY AND TENDERLY"

W hen al Qaeda came to the Dora District of Baghdad, they began harassing Shiite Muslims and Christians first, quickly escalating to violence and murder. Soon al Qaeda was attacking Sunni Muslims, sparking reprisals and revenge, inflaming the civil war. Hundreds of thousands of Christians and Muslims fled Baghdad. With Christian neighborhoods mostly emptied, and clergy being kidnapped and murdered, many Christian churches closed.

Despite being nearly destroyed by terrorist bombs, St. John's Church in Dora hung on until May 2007, when the violence and devastation of the neighborhood closed the church's doors.

But about six months after the launch of General Petraeus's new strategy to focus on securing the neighborhoods and rebuilding normal life, conditions had improved so dramatically that plans were afoot to reopen St. John's.

The most wonderful thing to see was how hard the Muslim neighbors worked to get the church reopened. Local Muslims invited me to see the reopening; they wanted Americans to know they protect Christians in their neighborhood.

A bishop came to St. John's on November 15, 2007, to celebrate the first mass since the church was shuttered. The bishop was welcomed by a crowd of locals who were joined at the service by soldiers from the 2-12 Infantry Battalion, many of whom had fought hard to secure these neighborhood streets. Members of the hard-fighting Iraqi Army 3rd Division from Nineveh province were also here for this special day.

Muslims mostly filled the front pews, Muslims who hoped their Christian friends and neighbors would see these photos and know how they are missed.

The Muslims worry that other people will take the homes of their Christian neighbors and that the Christians will never come back. And so they came to St. John's en masse, and they showed their faces, and they said, "Come back to Iraq. Come home. Tell the Christians to come home to their country Iraq."

FARAH DID NOT DIE IN VAIN

When little Farah heard the American Strykers, she dashed out of the house barefoot to wave at the Americans. Other kids had done the same. The soldiers tossed candy. The suicide-murderer driving the car bomb could have waited a couple of blocks to attack our soldiers, but instead rammed his car into the Stryker while about twenty kids were crowded around.

An Iraqi woman rushed little Farah out of the smoke and flames to sniper Sergeant Walt Gaya who, instead of pushing into sniper position, rushed Farah back to the medics. Major Mark Bieger saw Farah and scooped her up and rushed to a Stryker, but along the way Bieger kept stopping to hug her. Some of Farah's relatives loaded into the Stryker and they rushed to the hospital where Farah died.

Shortly after Farah's murder in May 2005, this picture, published all over Iraq and all over the world, had a devastating effect on the terrorists. Farah's death was not in vain.

CHAPTER EIGHT

Awakening in Anbar

'The social and political situation has deteriorated to a point that MNF [Multi-National Force] and ISF [Iraqi Security Forces] are no longer capable of militarily defeating the insurgency in al Anbar."

"Underlying this decline in stability is the near complete collapse of social order. . . ."

"The economy in western Iraq provides bare sustenance to the average citizen while enriching criminals, insurgents, and corrupt officials. The potential for economic revival appears to be nonexistent."

"[N]early all government institutions from the village to provincial level have disintegrated or have been thoroughly corrupted and infiltrated by al Qaeda in Iraq (AQI) or criminal/insurgent gangs. *Violence and criminality are now the principal driving factors behind daily life for most Anbar Sunni*; they commit violence or crime, avoid violence or crime through corruption and acquiescence, or become victims."

"AQI is the dominant organization of influence in al Anbar, surpassing nationalist insurgents, the Iraqi Government, and MNF in its ability to control the day-to-day life of the average Sunni."

"Although most al-Anbar Sunni dislike, resent, and distrust AQI, many increasingly see it as an inevitable part of daily life. . . ."

★   ★   ★

These quotes from a classified U.S. Marine Corps intelligence report describe the dire situation in Anbar province during the summer of 2006. The report, officially titled "The State of the Insurgency in Al Anbar," was written by Colonel Peter Devlin, a senior intelligence officer with the Marine Expeditionary Force based in Ramadi. Dated August 6, 2006, the report ignited the media when it was leaked to the press several weeks after Devlin completed it.

Headlines blared the bad news: "Grim Outlook Seen in West Iraq," "Situation Called Dire in West Iraq," and "U.S. Intel Report: Iraq's Anbar Province 'Politically Lost.'" As bits and pieces from the report were published, the province became known as "Anbar the Impossible." Anbar had been looking very bad during my trip there with CSM Mellinger in January 2007. Fallujah and Ramadi were one big shootout and bomb fest. Every mile we drove or walked I expected might be the last.

But when I went back four months later, large swaths of Anbar were more peaceful than just about any other area in Iraq, aside from the Kurdish north. The region that had once been the cause of a third of all U.S. combat deaths, the capital city that al Qaeda had brazenly announced to the world was its home in Iraq, was suddenly and without much media fanfare looking like a model for moving forward.

What happened?

The sheiks called it "Sahawah Al Anbar," the "Awakening of

Anbar," and with them the answer begins. To understand what happened in Anbar one must understand the sheiks who have governed this vast province that stretches from Baghdad west to the borders of Syria and Jordan for an unbroken thousand years.

★   ★   ★

In the beginning of the Iraq war, the people of Fallujah—the crucible of Anbar—showed little serious resistance. After all, this was the same region where the leaders of the largest tribe had been involved in a plot to assassinate Saddam Hussein in the 1990s. In Anbar, tribal allegiances are powerful social and political bonds. The sheiks at the head of each tribe control their people. Mohammed Fahdil, one of two Iraqi brothers whose writings on the blog "Iraq the Model" have been a continuous source of information and insight into Iraqi culture, explained the traditional role of the sheik for Sunni tribes in Anbar:

"The core of the struggle in Anbar is an old conflict of interests between clerics and tribal sheiks. The two groups competed for leadership of the society for centuries. Even though the sheik might show loyalty to the cleric, he still hides enmity for him; they're each other's nemesis. The difference between clerics and sheiks is huge; the first do not believe in negotiation and speak in terms of 'halal' and 'haram,' claiming to be representative of heaven's justice.

"Obviously you can't negotiate deals with God so as far as the clerics are concerned, society must follow them, without asking questions. By contrast, the tribal sheik was raised and taught to know how to lead productive negotiations. Tribal leaders have long played the role of judges to settle disputes among individuals within the tribe or between different tribes and when they do so they try to make sure that decisions are reached through consultation with the two sides of the dispute and would be acceptable to both as well. In other words a sheik has to be a good negotiator, willing to hear both sides of the story and convince them to make concessions in order to contain the problem and restore order—it's an important part of his job."

This is counterinsurgency 101. The sheiks were important leaders. Our Special Forces had wanted to develop ties with the sheiks early on, not just in Anbar but throughout Iraq. With rare exceptions that suggestion was rebuffed by conventional commanders. Even when the sheiks began making overtures toward us we ignored them because they came from people we considered irrelevant vestiges at best, terrorists at worst.

Thus our "welcome" in Anbar faded quickly. The sheiks who initially saw us as a necessary but obtrusive occupier began to see us as an enemy; we had invaded their country, then ignored or sidelined them.

The minor skirmishes that pockmarked the area in 2003 exploded early in 2004, and on the final day of March that year, four contractors were murdered and mutilated in Fallujah. Spokesmen for the killers called it an act of revenge, even justice. They called the murdered contractors mercenaries, while two charred American corpses dangled from what soldiers and marines now call "Blackwater Bridge."

At home Americans were enraged by images of the murderous mobs dancing while American bodies were burned and mutilated. Our military was ordered to punish the city. Nobody knows how many Iraqis died during the attacks on Fallujah, but the number is estimated to have been at least six hundred. Worse, though it has been widely reported that Americans have not lost a battle during this war, the attack was effectively repulsed with a full-spectrum enemy defense including a devastating media counterattack. The enemy fought ferociously on the ground, but their real victory was in the global media battle space. Fallujah I

(April 2004) gave the sheiks what they needed to galvanize an insurgency intent on driving Americans from Iraq. Explosions all over Iraq heralded the rise of Fallujah as the center of commerce for insurgents in the "City of Mosques." Throughout the summer and into the fall, the calls for the Americans to flatten Fallujah grew louder, until November 8, 2004, Operation Phantom Fury (Fallujah II) pummeled the city, igniting flames of resistance throughout key areas of Iraq. Al Qaeda had come from nothing in Iraq to becoming a factor after Fallujah I and the Abu Ghraib torture crimes that broke the same month. Then, after Fallujah II, al Qaeda was on course to become the most destructive force in the land due to its alliance with more organic and rational insurgent groups that had become increasingly radicalized by our blunders. Within days of the launch of Operation Phanton Fury, the city of Mosul fell to terrorists. Perhaps worse, a Sunni boycott of the first and most important national election was assured. And elsewhere Shia militias were growing to be one of the greatest threats to Iraqi stability and to U.S., British, and Iraqi forces.

The war in Anbar remained unabated through 2005 and 2006. During this time, Anbar became a special province for al Qaeda, a place in Iraq where they could establish and maintain a robust and largely unchallenged dominance, and a base from which they could launch attacks elsewhere. They made a training and R&R city out of Tal Afar in western Nineveh. Al Qaeda promised they would cast out the Americans and reward the people of Anbar with ministries in the new government. By early 2006, al Qaeda had three queens on the board. If they had known how to play the game, they could have crushed us in Iraq and won a strategic victory with global ramifications. Lucky for us their collective intellect did not match their savagery.

For al Qaeda, Iraq was just one front in their battle to humiliate and exhaust America—their strategy in Iraq was to provoke a civil war between Sunni and Shia. It was a tempting strategy, but al Qaeda militants are not smart insurgents. They know how to kill people and break things, but that's where their skill sets end. Once they have gained control of and responsibility for a territory, they can offer only terror. They do not know or care how to run a village, much less a city or nation. The locals came to view al Qaeda as degenerates and less than swine—using drugs, laying up sloppy drunk, using prostitutes, raping women and boys, and cutting off heads—while at the same time they are imposing strict morality laws on the locals. In 2007 in Baghdad, an army intelligence soldier told me that one of the best sources in their area was a gay al Qaeda member; when his al Qaeda lovers mistreated him, he would pass along intelligence to get them killed or captured.

A Spartacus Moment

Fortunately, the Special Forces teams who'd been in Anbar for several years had made inroads with some tribes. So when the people were disgusted with al Qaeda, the sheiks reached out to us, and this time we listened. According to retired Master Sergeant Chris Heim, a twenty-three-year veteran Special Forces soldier who was an integral player in the engagement with the Abu Nimr leadership in the Al Phurat region, southeast of Hit along the northeast bank of the Euphrates River: "The influence of the sheiks was immediately understood by SF, most of us sought rapport with the tribal sheiks since the early days of the war, mainly for local control of an area and then wider influence as the insurgency developed."

The Special Forces teams dealt with the sheiks "very carefully," Heim said. "It is all about rapport building. It is an arduous process and may take a long time and require many steps. SF are masters at this. It is done through financial gain, intimidation if need be, providing civil affairs projects, construction projects, medical clinics, etc. We saved [one sheik's] life on two occasions; he [was] an insulin-dependent diabetic and very non-compliant with his diet. He became septic from a gangrenous toe and we flew him to Baghdad to the U.S. military hospital and through personal connections with a U.S. Army vascular surgeon, had two femoral stints put in his legs and his toe amputated and infection cured, saving his life. That went a long way, trust me."

A crucial step was taken when Sheik Abu Ali Jassim was persuaded to cooperate with Special Forces to build and staff a police station for the city under the sheik's control. SF won his cooperation. The SF commander approached Sheik Jassim and told him he had funds to build and staff a police station, but wanted the sheik to tell him where it should go and to help hire men to serve on the police force. The sheik resisted at first, because in the past Iraqi Police recruits were typically required to work in places far removed from their hometowns. Sheik Jassim had no desire to send his young men away to protect another tribe while leaving their own families without protection. Special Forces assured him the recruits would work in the area. The recruitment drive was a success, and police were diligent in the protection of their community, according to Heim. Eventually Sheik Jassim began to talk to other tribes about the benefits of cooperating with the Americans. For this he was murdered by al Qaeda on August 21, 2006. Not content to silence the man's voice in this life, his murderers hid his body, leaving it to rot in a field rather than allowing for a rapid burial as stipulated by the Koran.

The murder and desecration was intended to intimidate and keep any other sheik from cooperating with Americans. It didn't work. Instead of frightening these men into submission, the act instead prompted what one marine colonel colorfully described as "A Spartacus Moment" for Sheik Abdul Sattar Buzaigh al-Rishawi

(Sheik Sattar) who stepped forward and in effect said, "I am Spartacus," putting himself in place of the murdered Sheik Jassim by publicly advocating cooperation with the Coalition.

It was Sheik Sattar who christened the movement "Sahawah Al Anbar." One by one the sheiks of Anbar stepped forward, declaring their allegiance to work with the Coalition to fight al Qaeda in Anbar and bring peace and security to their communities. Sheik Sattar's Spartacus Moment eventually inspired twenty-six of the thirty-one tribal leaders in Anbar to formally ally with the movement, certainly one of the most important events of the war, shifting its momentum almost overnight. With every tribal group that shifted allegiance, people shifted combat power, and other assets could be more finely focused against the holdouts and especially al Qaeda itself.

Sattar's emergence at the center of the movement he is credited with naming surprised many, including Chris Heim, who had known many of the sheiks in the region prior to their uprising against al Qaeda:

"I met Sheik Sattar once at a tribal council meeting with Sheik Hatem and Sheik Jubair and about thirty other sheiks. I was not overly impressed with him. He was a minor sheik as far as I know, more influential in the Ramadi area than Al Phurat. I think because of his media savvy and willingness to be in the limelight, he was chosen to be the spokesperson for the Awakening."

Sattar's media savvy brought him visits from ministry officials, and dignitaries, including a personal visit from President Bush on September 3, 2007. Sheik Sattar was killed in a car bomb attack near his home on September 13, 2007. But once again, the tactic backfired on AQI. Sheik Ahmed Abu Risha, who took his younger brother's place as head of the Awakening Council, said it best: "The martyrdom of Sattar will not affect this council, because every member of this council has the same beliefs and the same motivations, and this sad incident will not stop them from moving forward. Although they killed Sattar, there are a million Sattars in Anbar."

Bad for Business

COIN presents a complex and often unfamiliar set of missions and considerations for a military commander. In many ways, the conduct of counterinsurgency is counterintuitive to the traditional American view of war—although it has actually formed a substantial part of America's actual experience.

—*Counterinsurgency Field Manual*

As Sunni nationalist insurgents were cleaved away from their radical former allies and brought to our side—although they probably saw it as us coming to their side—we were increasingly side by side having tea and dinner in family homes. Our soldiers began to understand more about the tribal structure and its role in Iraqi society. They'd ask, "Hey, what tribe does that guy belong to?" knowing this could be important to know.

When American leaders finally sat down and talked to the sheiks, it became clear that most sheiks were reasonable people (with a trick or two up their sleeves) with whom we could do business. For sheiks are businessmen. Ultimately the sheiks of Anbar turned against al Qaeda because al Qaeda was bad for business.

The conflict in Iraq is often cast as either a battle between good and evil, or as a clash of religious ideologies, filling cemeteries with brave souls eager to die for their beliefs. Anbar was awakened by the less lofty imperative that peace is better for business, and self-interest is a more reliable motive for cooperation than self-sacrifice.

The insurgency in Anbar began with a practical alliance between the sheiks, the insurgents, and al Qaeda, all opposing the U.S. for different reasons. We got our second chance in Anbar when it became clear that everyone but al Qaeda would be better off doing business with the Coalition.

The sheiks are not the Rotary Club. There is no oil in Anbar province. The place is mostly desert—and borders. The business of many of the tribes was smuggling, which meant that doing business with some of the sheiks was like doing business with trash haulers in Jersey or longshoremen on the Baltimore piers.

Iraq is a corrupt country. As Chris Heim put it: "Remember in Iraq, after thirty plus years of Saddam there is a deeply embedded culture of corruption, then add the Arab culture of corruption. We did our best to recognize and discourage it."

Some of the money we pump into Iraq will buy big sheiks big cars. Some will be stolen by politicians in Baghdad. But some will go to rebuild their ravaged cities. Some will be wasted, but an Abrams tank blasted into oblivion with a full crew of American soldiers inside is a far more serious loss. It's better to buy water pumps, knowing some of the money will be pumped away, and have the sheiks on our side. In the same way, it would have been better to keep many of the Ba'athists and Iraqi Army on payroll, rather than turning them into a fierce enemy in the streets. Iraq has been a great expense since the first Gulf War. In Anbar during the spring of 2007, for the first time I saw that expense becoming an investment.

★   ★   ★

When General Petraeus took command in early 2007 he had the diplomatic and political skills to take full advantage of "the cleaving" that was already underway. (People talk about "the surge." But there was something else that happened: "the cleaving." We hacked a lot of the groups apart from one another.) During the fall and winter of 2006, our military had already progressed substantially in transforming how it conducted the war. Heavy-handed tactics were mostly gone, replaced instead by a multi-dimensional counterinsurgency strategy rolled out simultaneously with tightly targeted kinetic battles.

The army was learning. Yet the marines adapted faster and seemed poised to win the war in their battle space. In fact, army officers frequently told me that nobody was more successfully morphing to meet the challenges of this war faster than the marines. Of course, army officers who complimented the marines would always say, "But that didn't come from me." Yet it was U.S. Army Special Forces and other less visible organizations that brought the first serious inroads to Anbar.

Knowing this made an offer to embed with marines in Anbar irresistible. So I headed out to Fallujah and requested to speak with Colonel Richard Simcock II, the U.S. Marine Corps Commanding Officer for Regimental Combat Team 6, whose responsibility included Fallujah.

Through a Window, Clearly

Success in COIN operations requires small-unit leaders agile enough to transition among many types of missions and able to adapt to change. They must be able to shift through a number of activities from nation building to combat and back again in days, or even hours. . . . Adaptable leaders observe the rapidly changing situation, identify its key characteristics, ascertain what has to be done in consultation with subordinates, and determine the best method to accomplish the mission.

—*Counterinsurgency Field Manual*

If you are going on a combat mission and soldiers have not cleaned all their windows to a sparkle, do not go with them. Soldiers with dirty windows are not watching for tiny wires in the road, nor are they scanning rooftops. They are talking about women, football, and the cars they will buy when they get home. I will not go into combat with soldiers with dirty windows.

I also look at the state of their weapons and ammunition. Does the machine-gunner have lubricant? Before going out with them, does someone tell me what to do if there is any drama? Or do they just drag me into combat like a sack of potatoes? It's usually very simple. A platoon sergeant will say, "Sir, you stay next to me and do what I tell you. We'll probably get you back alive." Most combat soldiers fall into the "ready, prepared, and alert" category.

Likewise, I first look at media relations. In counterinsurgency, commanders who are afraid of the press cannot win. Dealing with the press is just a reality, like the weather. We would never put a commander in the field who refused to make plans for fighting in the cold or heat. It's the same with the press: hostile, friendly, or neutral, it has to be dealt with.

Within an hour of my landing in Fallujah, the Marine Public Affairs had me set up in a secure trailer with a live Internet connection. They even provided extra AA and AAA batteries. I had been trying for weeks to get new batteries, but I had not told these marines that. They anticipated the need. The Public Affairs officer said I could have anything in the room. There were books and magazines. There was even a little refrigerator stocked with water and snacks. I was astounded. Sometimes it took days just to get an Internet connection at the big army base in Baghdad, or to get a memo to get into a dining facility. Days of lost time, wasted for nothing, and forever.

Before I arrived in mid-May, the Iraqi Army and Police had conducted a Combined Medical Exercise in the village of Falahat, where Iraqi doctors saw about two hundred villagers. A couple of days later, the Iraqi Police opened a police station at the Falahat train station. That was about the same time I went out to stay with a small team of marines who were assigned as MiTT 8 (Military Training Team 8). MiTTs are familiar territory for me; this is a vintage Special Forces concept used the world over. Special Forces teams like the one led by Chris Heim had been out here for years laying the foundation so the Awakening could be more than a photo-op.

The men of MiTT 8 were living along with their Iraqi protégées in filthy shipping containers on a highway. Several months prior they had been attacked by a car bomb. While I was traveling to their location with marines in a Humvee (with sparkling glass) some Falahat villagers went to the new police station to report the presence of a culprit they knew was emplacing bombs on the road. This was only days after the station opened.

Sometimes it happens that quickly. Within days of opening the station, people spoke up. The Iraqi Police called the tip in to the Iraqi Army who were living with the marines of MiTT 8. The Iraqi Army in turn told Marine Captain Koury, whose Command Operations Center was conjoined with the Iraqi Army unit. Finally, Captain Koury told Staff Sergeant Rakene Lee to take care of the situation.

The Humvee pulled up to the small MiTT 8 compound, where we met SSG Lee, dressed for combat. He was to lead the mission to the suspected bomb site. He saw me in the backseat and asked who I was. "A writer," I answered. Lee got in and we drove toward the suspected bomb.

We stopped short of the location, a culvert and tunnel beneath a four-lane highway. Two other IEDs had previously been placed there. SSG Lee got out of the Humvee and I followed, though apparently he hadn't expected me to get out. He didn't order me back in.

The Iraqi Police arrived. Meanwhile, some Iraqis caught the suspected bomber elsewhere, and brought him to the marines. While all this was unfolding we headed back up to the road to search for the bomb. As SSG Lee went in to clear the culvert and tunnel, I saw marks from a recent explosion on a nearby wall. The entrances to the culvert were easy for the enemy to reach unobserved. Mines, bombs, or other booby traps could have been planted. Lee could have ordered one of the Iraqis to clear the culvert, and I'm sure an Iraqi would have done so. Many were very courageous. But Lee was mentoring these men, and without hesitation, he entered the culvert himself to check it out.

People at home want to know what our soldiers and marines are doing in Iraq, and the only way to tell their story is to follow them. So deep inside the culvert, I crawled on all fours behind SSG Lee. The day was hot. The body armor made it hotter.

"I only met you for the first time like twenty minutes ago," I said as we crawled down the tunnel. "What's your name, Staff Sergeant?"

"Staff Sergeant Lee, sir."

"United States Marine Corps."

"Semper Fi," he said, and kept crawling.

The tunnel was clear.

An Iraqi soldier entered the culvert from the other side. Up on top, they searched a fresh hole near the location of the two previous bombs, but found nothing. Lee wanted to go talk with the police at the Falahat station; he and I left the small group of marines and headed back to the station with the Iraqis.

Three suspects had been detained. SSG Lee took two of the prisoners and the Iraqis took the other. Lee's two were shepherds whose proximity had made them natural suspects, but he wasn't certain they had been involved. Their hands were not bound, but they were blindfolded and told to keep their hands behind their backs. They were given water and treated respectfully. Eventually they were released.

SSG Lee made sure the Iraqis treated the detainees well during transport, and when we returned to the tiny base, Captain Koury told the marines not to leave any of the prisoners alone with the Iraqis. The Iraqis can be rough on prisoners—the culture can be rough—but the marines' mentoring seemed to be working.

At the station SSG Lee had stressed to the police that we needed statements from the witnesses reporting the bomb, so people from Falahat came in and gave written statements. The statements that Lee had insisted the police get from villagers led to the detaining of a "Mr. R." and raids were planned based on information he provided.

The Persuasive Power of Character

Before long, I understood why army officers had been telling me the marines were more advanced in counterinsurgency. These marines were doing vintage Special Forces work and had a flair for it. They were even studying Arabic in their filthy little compound. It might have been lightweight study, but they were showing the Iraqis they were making the effort. The Iraqis appreciated it.

One of the most important things I saw was that Iraqi soldiers and police constantly emulated marines and soldiers. When he got back from missions, SSG Lee worked out. The Iraqis would watch him and start doing their own exercises. Lee was just being himself, and the young Iraqis wanted to be like him.

Iraqis in every province I traveled all responded to strong leadership. It's a cultural touchstone. A man like Rakene Lee was not someone they could overlook. Physically, the man was amazingly strong. But even more amazing was the strength of his moral fiber. Whatever the man talked, he walked. After all of al Qaeda's false promises, the people here had learned a hard lesson about the true value of character.

During my time in Anbar, I saw how much the Iraqis respected Rakene Lee and the other marines who were all courageous, tactically competent, measured, and constantly telling even the Iraqis to go easy on other Iraqis. By showing that the strongest soldier is also disciplined, just, and compassionate, soldiers like SSG Lee were winning the moral high ground in Iraq and devastating al Qaeda. I saw an Iraqi Army lieutenant named Hamid treating prisoners with respect, because he had seen American soldiers do it. Lieutenant Hamid, in his young twenties, seemed to watch every move of the marines and try to emulate them. I saw qualities the first day in Hamid that shouted out to me, "This man can become a great leader." But Hamid was still a young lion in need of mentoring, and SSG Rakene Lee was doing a particularly fine job of this.

Lieutenant Hamid was a Shia from Sadr City, but was working in mostly Sunni Anbar province. I found Lieutenant Hamid to be courageous, intelligent, and endowed with natural leadership abilities. Hamid made a point of asking me to take his photo. He said he wanted al Qaeda to come and look for him.

One night, after a long day out in the sun, when we were all exhausted, I sat talking with Hamid. He told me how he'd lost his girlfriend of two years. She'd been studying banking in Baghdad, and when Hamid told her he wanted to join the Iraqi Army, she replied that if he did so, she would break up with him. He said it was a very tough decision. Hamid's father had been a soldier in Saddam's army, as had other relatives, some of whom died fighting.

When he told his girlfriend that he must go to the Iraqi Army, she left him. He told me, with remarkable sadness, "Women are crazy."

For two weeks Hamid was so sick he could hardly eat. Finally he went to a hospital and a doctor gave him an IV. When Hamid returned to duty, he decided he would be a soldier for life and might not ever get married. And then he said it again, "Women are crazy," but this time we laughed.

Taking an American off the street and building him into a competent marine or soldier takes a long time. It's no different with Iraqis. But it was happening.

I recall one day when it was just SSG Lee and me along with dozens of Iraqis, some of whom clearly were insurgents being brought into the fold. Lieutenant Hamid was there with us, and we were far away from backup. And so there was young Hamid the Shia from Sadr City, surrounded by Sunni insurgents. Every time we interacted with Iraqi civilians or prisoners, Hamid would watch SSG Rakene Lee, and he would emulate him. If Hamid survives, one day he might become a general, and he likely will remember those marines who treated Iraqis so well.

CHAPTER NINE

High Noon

The air was blowing hot and dry through Hit on the morning of May 29, 2007. The sounds of a busy marketplace filled the air as LTC Doug Crissman, commander of the Task Force 2-7 Infantry, and I strolled the crowded downtown streets. Situated on the western bank of the Euphrates, Hit was a spot of green in the desert. The temperature had risen steadily as days melted into the mirage of summer; haze shimmered off the thermometer that read 115° F. Our several-mile walk through the market—a veritable shopping mall for the area—was filled with men, women, and children of all ages, including one rotund boy furiously rushing to slurp his ice cream before it dripped away in the heat.

Five months earlier, Hit had been one of the hottest little battlegrounds of the war. Today, we had only two soldiers as guards. The people were busy, though many waved and smiled. A few asked to talk with LTC Crissman, who stopped now and then to engage in conversations. Compared to my last visit to Anbar earlier in the year, this uneventful amble was change of staggering scale.

Many people in Hit attributed the resurrection of their city in large part to the courage of Ibrahim Hamid Jaza—known as General Hamid—the district Iraqi police chief who had taken an aggressive stand against the al Qaeda in Iraq terrorists. The people of Anbar were soon intensely disgusted with al Qaeda's hypocrisy and severely angered by their brutality. The people wanted al Qaeda gone. There was killing to be done.

General Hamid took the lead and went for al Qaeda throats, showing that the terrorists were also vulnerable. Some soldiers in Task Force 2-7 began to refer to the general as "Buford Pusser," because Hamid literally carried a big stick. Al Qaeda wasn't laughing. They beheaded one of Hamid's sons on a soccer field in the center of Hit in 2005.

Although rumors of Hamid's shady past and possible corruption had always trailed him, Hamid was a hero to many Americans and Iraqis. While most men cast down their eyes in the face of true terrorism, Hamid had stood strong and faced the al Qaeda devils that polluted the winds with their breath and poisoned the earth with their touch.

That afternoon it would become LTC Crissman's job to arrest a hero without losing what had been gained in Hit. The tragic story of General Hamid is a perfect example of the paradoxes encountered in a values-driven counterinsurgency.

The Right Man for the Job

Long before Colonel Devlin's intelligence report on the disaster of Anbar leaked the bad news to the world that Anbar was helpless, many in the U.S. military had written off Anbar province as hopeless. But some special operations folks I spoke with disagreed.

Beginning in 2005, the Special Forces soldiers of the 5th SFG ODA 545 (Operational Detachment/Alpha: the technical name for a Special Forces A team) had worked in the Al Phurat region of Anbar province to engage the Abu Nimr tribe with the Iraqi security forces to start the Desert Protector (DP) program. The Abu Nimr tribe, in addition to being one of the largest and most influential in the province, had also been involved in a plot to assassinate Saddam Hussein in the 1990s. Tribal leaders could see the benefits of a strong and diverse Iraqi Army and police force, and many tribe members were attracted by the prospect of paying jobs. Nevertheless, prior recruitment efforts had not been remarkable. At that time, recruits had to leave their homes and work in other parts of Iraq. Given the increasing al Qaeda barbarity, few men were willing to leave their families unprotected. That's where the Desert Protectors would come in.

One of the Desert Protector platoon's first and most visible achievements was to protect their fellow tribesmen who wished to vote in the December elections of 2005. In January 2006, Master Sergeant Heim's ODA 182 relieved ODA 545, continuing to assist with the DP program. He writes:

"The Desert Protectors escorted over a thousand Abu Nimr men to Hit—without incident—in order to vote during the December 15, 2005, national elections, which led to a significant change of attitude in Al Phurat.

"Prior to that, men were afraid to leave Al Phurat to join the army, because they feared for the safety of their families during the time they would be gone.

"With the DPs on hand, men began volunteering for the Iraqi Army by the hundreds, because they felt confident that their fellow tribesmen in the DPs would keep their families safe while they were gone."

As recruiting picked up it was essential that the security forces earn the trust of the citizens. As LTC Crissman remarked, "I have told my Iraqi partners many times that we feel like we spend half our time teaching, coaching, and mentoring them to improve their systems and processes and half our time policing corrupt behavior. Many of the intelligence tips we get from local citizens come from citizens who don't trust the police and won't bring them intelligence. It's getting better, but only as we help the Iraqis find professional officers who are able to resist the temptations that come with power and influence and coach and enforce the same behavior from their subordinates."

General Hamid was the obvious man to serve as district chief for the new force. Hamid was in his late forties, with adult children (several of whom were murdered by AQI), and he was well known in the region. He was from a subtribe of the Abu Nimr. Among his tribesmen, Hamid had a great deal of what Heim called "wasta," or respect. Although Hamid completed only eight years of formal schooling, he was streetwise and a strong leader. Very early in their efforts to engage the Abu Nimr tribe, Heim's ODA approached Hamid to be "an information conduit" and found him reliable and competent. "Hamid provided information on al Qaeda in Iraq, throughout the region, even into Ramadi, Fallujah, and Baghdad. He had access to everywhere and was vetted pretty quickly." Hamid's adroitness with the press had brought positive attention to the leaders in Anbar.

Now though, some local officials who had once regarded Hamid as a hero were beginning to fear him. There were claims he was committing murders, releasing some detainees for money, abusing other detainees, making deals with various insurgent groups including selling weapons and ammunition, and condoning prostitution in Hit.

Tribal politics may also have been a factor, at least for some of the sheiks. MSG Heim, whose deployment had ended before LTC

Crissman arrived with 2-7 Infantry, would later tell me that there was a long-standing "palpable" animosity between Hamid and one sheik in particular. Heim says, "Hamid was an outspoken critic of the sheiks and their influence, calling them corrupt and inefficient." (A common complaint in Iraq.)

Even though Iraqi and American officials understood that Hamid was a crucial aspect of the recent success against al Qaeda, they became convinced Hamid was out of control. But even with his flaws, Hamid still flew on a carpet woven of respect. Someone floated the idea of giving Hamid an early retirement, complete with a medal and a ceremony. But others thought Hamid was too smart, too proud, and too dangerous to be allowed to become a free agent. The last thing Anbar province needed was another power broker working outside the system, and especially one with Hamid's cunning and contacts. Certain sheiks had their own reasons for wanting Hamid gone. The Americans were sure from their own intelligence that Hamid was engaged in criminal activity.

Crissman was also mindful that Iraqis have their own sense of time and a limited store of patience. Knowing that the Coalition had operated hand-in-hand with General Hamid, local Iraqis would likely interpret our continued tolerance of the situation as a sign that we were in cahoots, condoned, or at least turned a blind eye. The problem was further complicated because many people, Americans and Iraqis, actually liked Hamid, when he was on good behavior.

For several days as I accompanied Crissman, he circulated throughout his area of Anbar, meeting with sheiks, imams, city council members, a mayor, and Iraqi policemen. Invariably, concerns about General Hamid's conduct came out. Each meeting made it more clear that many Iraqis wanted Hamid gone. And they wanted us to be the ones to arrest him. Anbar had not been turned over to provincial Iraqi control, so the task would properly fall to the Coalition. The CIA, the military, and the Iraqi government all agreed that Hamid had gone rogue but also felt a move against him could go badly. We needed to act carefully.

A secret mission called Operation Police Call was planned. Hamid was to be arrested. Senior Coalition and Iraqi leadership including Prime Minister Maliki were to be apprised of the arrest when and if it was ordered.

On the morning of May 29, however, there was no plan and no orders to arrest General Hamid that day.

Instead, Crissman's agenda that morning involved a meeting with a number of sheiks and police chiefs on another police issue. There were more than five hundred police hiring slots to fill. Crissman had been making great effort to distribute the slots over various tribes and neighborhood boundaries to increase the number of stakeholders in the security program. The dominant Abu Nimr tribe was trying to grab too many slots. While we were inside a police chief's office haggling with the chiefs and the sheiks over details, perhaps a hundred aspirants were waiting outside for screening. While Crissman was drawing pie charts to illustrate (through his interpreter) a fair mix of tribes and regions for a particular police unit, a ruckus started outside among the recruits.

I pulled on body armor and a helmet and walked outside to a chaotic scene: job seekers carried assault rifles; there were machine guns mounted on Iraqi trucks; there was pushing and intense yelling and some of the men began cocking their weapons.

I waded through the crowd of angry men to another group of American soldiers and asked them what was happening. Nobody exactly knew, but I saw some of our guys trying to isolate the troublemakers. One of Crissman's soldiers walked a screaming Iraqi man behind a Humvee and gave him ice-cold water and told him to calm down, which worked for a while, until another man carrying a machine gun started screaming again. One of LTC

Crissman's young soldiers told the new screamer in colorful terms that if he didn't back off he was going to get handcuffed.

The angry mob scene had formed because of a shortage of hiring orders, which translated to fewer paychecks, which was what Crissman and the Iraqis inside were haggling about. The men needed jobs. Although the situation was tense, my sense was that we were seeing more bravado than imminent bloodshed. Iraqi police commanders waded into the crowd and began calming people down.

Meanwhile, events were accelerating on the Hamid front. That morning, an Iraqi policeman named Major Walid had gone to General Hamid's office. Walid was the head investigator in charge of a team of about eight to twelve police officers. His team worked closely with the Hit district judge to help secure warrants prior to arrests or searches. Their broad mandate had them also investigating individuals who were alleged to have committed misdemeanors, felonies, or terrorist-related activity. Major Walid had been summoned to Hamid's office that morning, because one of his investigations was starting to hit close to home.

Walid was investigating a serious allegation against Hamid. Both the Coalition and the Iraqis believed Hamid was harboring Zayid Yusef Jarwan, a known terrorist who operated in Ramadi. Hamid might have released Jarwan in return for a bribe. Evidence also showed that Hamid was involved in abusing detainees and mistreating women. When Walid went to Hamid's office that morning, Hamid demanded that Walid drop the investigation. Then, as we were soon to find out, Hamid beat Walid.

By 12:00 noon, the Iraqi-American Joint Coordination Center (JCC) was getting reports that fliers were being distributed around Hit complaining that Hamid was freeing insurgents for money. The fliers called on Coalition forces to do something. Other fliers, believed to be coming from Hamid's side, claimed the allegations were false. Iraqis seem to have a natural knack for press battles.

Around 1:00 P.M., two members of the Hit City Council arrived at the JCC demanding that the Coalition do something, fearful that others would take business into their own hands. The council members said that people in the city did not want to attack the police general, but they had had enough. Without intervention, a mob intent on lynching Hamid would surely confront an armed contingent of his supporters, and American forces would be involved in the crossfire. Nobody needed that. Aside from the violence, it would also undermine Crissman's daily efforts to instill confidence that there would be a rule of law in Hit and that no one—not even the chief of police—was above it.

While these events were unfolding, Crissman headed our small patrol of Humvees north on Route Trout along the Euphrates to Hamid's office at the Hit district headquarters. The idea then was not to arrest Hamid, but Crissman wanted to show his face and keep up contact. While en route, Crissman got word on his command radio of the dueling fliers and the beating of Major Walid.

As we pulled into the police station, seven trucks filled with heavily armed Iraqi men were heading out. Although I'd been in many dozens of Iraqi police stations, this was the first time I could recall entering a station and having the distinct impression that a firefight with the police was imminent. Our soldiers, who knew these police because they had spent much time with them, also seemed ready for a fight. No weapons were pointed. This was in contrast to the ruckus earlier that morning when the recruits screamed and cocked their weapons, which seemed more like a way to pound the table than to start a real gun battle. Now the quiet, ready men on both sides buzzed with high voltage: DANGER.

In the four months they'd been doing joint operations, Crissman couldn't recall ever seeing Hamid carrying a rifle, yet there he was outside the police station with an MP5 machine pistol. Police were on the roof with machine guns and AK-47s. Crissman believed that Hamid was taking his posse out to confront the people who were gathering to confront him: seven truckloads of armed Iraqi police, with more on the rooftops as backup. We were outnumbered at least two to one.

When Crissman met Hamid on the ground outside of their vehicles he calmly exchanged the usual hugs and handshakes. Trying to vent the pressure, Crissman smiled and asked where everyone was going. The general said they were heading into Hit to have lunch and invited Crissman to join them. Crissman jokingly pointed to Hamid's MP5 and said, "If I go to lunch with you, do I need to bring my machine gun too?" Crissman's interpreter translated and there were smiles and laughter, until Crissman asked if he could talk with Hamid inside his office.

Unbeknownst to anyone on the scene, including me, as soon as we rolled up and saw those seven truckloads of Hamid's men, Crissman had called for backup from the platoon-sized QRF (Quick Reaction Force), who were all running to their Bradleys as we headed in to Hamid's office. No one but Crissman knew what was about to happen. Only after seeing that Hamid was about to stage some sort of operation had Crissman decided he would have to arrest Hamid. He also secretly called his executive officer on the radio to let him know that a Coalition Force was about to detain an Iraqi police chief—something that normally required advance notification and permission.

After about fifteen minutes of discussion in Hamid's office, we heard the Bradleys rumbling outside. I knew something was going down, but I still had no idea what. Watching Crissman deal with Hamid, I didn't get any clues. The Bradley company commander, CPT Dan Fitch, entered Hamid's office, and sat in on the meeting for some minutes. Crissman and Fitch were clearly using some kind of verbal code; I could tell that much, though it seemed Hamid did not notice. But I had no idea what they were telling each other. Soon Fitch left the room.

Inside the office, while still talking with Crissman, General Hamid unslung his submachine gun and propped it up against the wall. I noticed that General Hamid's pistol holster was unsnapped, making the weapon virtually effortless to draw.

Fitch returned to the office and handed Crissman a note. Suddenly, LTC Crissman asked me if I would photograph him and Hamid together. Iraqi Police and Army officers are keen to have their photographs taken, particularly with American forces. Photos of Hamid covered the wall behind his desk. I pulled out my camera. Crissman stood calmly beside Hamid and smiled as I snapped a couple of photos. After the last photo, Crissman deftly slipped Hamid's pistol out of his unsnapped holster. Crissman smiled and said, "This hurts me more than it hurts you, but I'm going to need you to come with me, General."

Hamid seemed confused at first, as if his friend were just admiring his Glock pistol. Hamid kept smiling as Crissman politely said that Hamid was to be detained.

Acting solely on his own and with no direct orders from above, but seeing that a bloodbath was about to happen, Crissman had pulled a plan out of the sky. While Crissman had continued discussing seemingly important issues with General Hamid, soldiers from Task Force 2-7 Infantry had been outside, quietly separating Iraqi police, disarming, and flex-cuffing them. No shots were fired. No punches were thrown. Crissman managed to arrest an entire police station by using a photo-op to distract a proud, some might say vain, general just long enough to disarm him.

Not all the police were taken, just Hamid's personal team, which included forteen men and General Hamid. When Hamid asked for a cigarette, an American soldier offered him one, careful to keep his own pistol away from Hamid's reach.

General Hamid was not actually a prisoner of war. His problems were with the Iraqi government, not ours. As it turned out, Hamid was actually a colonel, but he had claimed the rank for so long that everybody called him general.

Tensions at the station were contained, but Crissman still needed to ensure that conditions remained peaceful in the area. After dropping off the prisoners at a small American base nearby, Crissman continued to the Joint Coordination Center, where he had asked all the police chiefs in the area to assemble.

Crissman told the police chiefs the truth about what had happened and what needed to happen next. The chiefs, nervous at first, soon responded with cooperation. Already, information of a possible reprisal attack surfaced. Crissman asked the chiefs to help him detain a couple men who might deliver reprisals. Iraqi authorities detained the men within hours. Crissman had already ordered the reinforcement of all the Iraqi police stations in the city as well as the bridge across the Euphrates. A three-day curfew would give folks time to calm down, and time to get the truth out about what happened.

Our own generals and Iraqi officials needed to know about the arrest, but Crissman also realized that his most immediate problem was making sure everyone in Hit realized that this was not a coup or precipitous action done at the whim of the Coalition, but had been requested by the region's leaders. At the same time, most of the local leaders knew of the tensions between Hamid and tribal leaders, and it was important to reassure them immediately that Hamid was not being summarily jailed and that his safety and well being were not in question. So instead of heading back to base after dropping off the prisoners, Crissman kept meeting with local leaders and reassuring them. These meetings were as important as the arrests that probably avoided a bloodbath.

During an emergency meeting of the Hit City Council, at least one council member argued that Hamid was still a hero, but most agreed with Crissman's action and thanked him. As the meeting drew to a close, Crissman reiterated that he had not arrested General Hamid for himself or the Coalition, but for the people of Hit. They all nodded in agreement and support and there were a few "shukrans" (thank yous) muttered. Crissman then said he needed to call his boss, since he had just arrested an Iraqi general and some people might be a little upset about that. The council members seemed stunned. I was stunned, having not realized until that moment that Crissman had simply seen the clear shot and taken it.

When Crissman told the Iraqi leaders he might be in real trouble for arresting Hamid, he joked that he might need a place to stay. The council burst into laughter, with members saying he could live in Hit. In a way, he already did.

Crissman summarized the rise and fall of General Hamid for me months after the arrest:

"Our Task Force cleared the city of Hit and its surrounding insurgent sanctuaries inside of thirty days from our arrival. We would not have been successful if it weren't for BG Hamid. He helped us achieve things we would not have attempted on our own. He struck fear in the enemy, and he commanded respect from his IPs and the population. He was the Buford Pusser of Hit. He carried a big stick and wasn't afraid to use it. He was THE right choice to fight AQI and partner with Coalition forces to re-turn stability to Hit . . . but his power got the best of him in the end . . . and once there were no more terrorists for him to kill, he had difficulty being a professional policeman and responsible member of the community."

Iraqis respect men of action and conviction and they recognize and respond to leadership. Hamid was a man of action and
was loved for a time. Rumors of his corruption were a blow to
many people. Finally, local leaders sought out a man like Crissman, a man they could trust because he had shown them leadership, character, and restraint.

Lack of restraint nearly cost us the war during the first couple
years. Leadership, character, and restraint are why we are winning
the war in Iraq—now.

CHAPTER TEN

Operation Arrowhead Ripper

W hen an insurgency reaches a certain level of success, it must plant its flag. This means controlling territory, setting up a new government, providing some level of services to the civilians. The Taliban do it in Afghanistan. Hezbollah does it in Lebanon. The attempt to govern was al Qaeda's hamartia. Sadism in the name of their god, rampant drug use, wild-eyed greed, and just general stupidity were more in their line. Animals like al Qaeda cannot govern humans in Iraq. An insurgency needs the people and must provide for the people. Al Qaeda went to great effort to destroy Iraqi physical and social infrastructures, while insurgent groups such as the 1920 Revolution Brigades excluded infrastructure targets, schools, and tended to avoid massive attacks on civilians. By 2006, it was becoming clear to large numbers of Iraqis that al Qaeda did not care what happened to Iraqis and Iraq. If al Qaeda had any coherent plan, it was for Iraq to cease to exist; al Qaeda wanted to turn Iraq into the base of their worldwide caliphate. When

Iraqis figured this out, they became, let's say, non-compliant with al Qaeda. Unfortunately, however, in the interim, al Qaeda received so much training and military knowledge from Iraqi Former Regime Elements, that AQI had morphed into something especially deadly, and those skills were transferring back to Afghanistan, for instance. While I was in Afghanistan in 2006, there were two close-by suicide bomb attacks in a town that had never before experienced such attacks, and the roadside bombs clearly were mimicking successes in Iraq. Al Qaeda had not been here in Iraq before, now they had become strong. Yet if al Qaeda were defeated in Iraq, the defeat would be strategic.

In the areas under their control in Iraq, al Qaeda conducted military operations, torture, incarceration, and executions. There was no education except combat training and no civil affairs other than sharia courts, criminal activities, and sabotage. AQI ideas of governance were so crude and cruel they quickly lost any goodwill they might have had with the local populace, all while the Coalition was rebounding from our mistakes of 2003–2004. Month by month, AQI was ceding moral high ground—they didn't think they needed it; they had their god and their guns—and we were taking every inch we could get. Even the Taliban in Afghanistan were more advanced in governance than al Qaeda. A friend of mine has a contracting company in Afghanistan, and when one of his employees was kidnapped, he reported the kidnapping to American and Afghan officials who did nothing. When he raised it with the Taliban, the employee was released without ransom unharmed, though they kept his truck. The Taliban can be fundamentalist savages, but they do actually have a sense for governance. And the Taliban are a limited, local issue. Al Qaeda is an infectious cult of nihilist murderers with global aspirations and global reach.

In June 2007, while I was with an infantry company called C-52 in Baghdad as they conducted final planning and rehearsals for Arrowhead Ripper to rip al Qaeda out of Baqubah, terrorists struck again at the great Al-Askariya Mosque in Samarra, Iraq. The golden dome of the mosque had been destroyed in a February 2006 bombing in one of al Qaeda's more dramatic attempts to provoke sectarian violence, but two lone minarets had been left standing. The June 2007 flattening of the minarets attributed to al Qaeda did result in some reprisals in nearby Babil province and rippled as far as Basra. But the aftershocks were not as widespread and open-necked as expected. Many Sunni and Shia now seemed to understand that they were being deliberately provoked by al Qaeda into a civil war. Sunni were starting to catch on to what a future with al Qaeda might look like.

As the Sunni Awakening drove al Qaeda out of Anbar province, they fled to places like Baghdad, Arab Jabour, and to Diyala province, a region where the Diyala River flows down from the city of Baqubah into the outskirts of Baghdad. Al Qaeda now declared their caliphate HQ in Iraq would not be Ramadi, as planned (along with other places that failed, such as Tal Afar), but instead would now be Baqubah. To launder the stink of the name al Qaeda, they renamed their alliance, several times, and created a hastily crafted "constitution" and a more impressive Web site, and set up shop in Iraq's breadbasket. For those few people who were paying attention, al Qaeda could be darkly humorous to watch; they were like Charles Manson—who dreamed about a civil war in the U.S.—trying to change his image with a twenty-minute makeover. Al Qaeda would pause to get a new haircut, then go back to writing on walls with human blood: Helter Skelter.

Baqubah, the capital of Diyala province, is a city of two hundred thousand people only thirty-five miles from Baghdad. Diyala is ethnically mixed and therefore more prone to sectarian violence than either Sunni-dominated Anbar or the Shia south. As the civil war that al Qaeda always wanted became harder to sustain elsewhere, in part because the Shia and Sunni had increasingly segregated themselves and so many displaced people had fled Iraq, and in part because al Qaeda was so discredited in Anbar, it seemed Diyala might be more fruitful ground. Diyala borders Iran, which was alleged to be aiding both Shia and Sunni insurgents, as well as transporting weapons and fighters into Iraq. Baqubah's proximity to Baghdad made it all the more important for the American side because terrorists sheltered in Baqubah were causing havoc in Baghdad. In early summer 2007, insurgents veritably owned Baqubah. Our folks were sustaining serious losses.

As in Anbar, al Qaeda quickly tarnished its name in Baqubah by the same brutal tactics: murdering of children; beheadings; drug use—all while imposing harsh punishments on Iraqi civilians found guilty of violating morality laws. Al Qaeda's sharia court sanctioned the amputation of a person's two "smoking fingers," or even called for the execution of those who violated anti-smoking laws. Most Iraqi men smoke. After an American unit cleared an apartment complex in Baqubah, the residents didn't ask for food and water, but cigarettes. In other parts of Baqubah, people would celebrate the routing of al Qaeda by lighting up.

Other al Qaeda in Iraq edicts included beatings for men who refused to grow beards and corporal punishment for obscene sexual suggestiveness, including such "loose" behavior as carrying tomatoes and cucumbers in the same bag. The judges who administer sharia law and issue fatwas are called muftis. These fatwas were not embraced by most Iraqis, and tainted the muftis.

Al Qaeda, trying to foment civil war, had so overplayed its bloody hand that it was becoming a common enemy of the Iraqi people and a basis for Iraqi unity. The time had come to retake Baqubah.

Operation Arrowhead Ripper

The night before Operation Arrowhead Ripper began, I wrote the dispatch "Be Not Afraid," which opened this book. The risks, for everyone and the entire war, were enormous. Even with all the success we had seen in Anbar, we had not fought a large-scale fixed battle since Fallujah. Operation Arrowhead Ripper and Operation Phantom Thunder (the larger operation of which Arrowhead Ripper was a part) were going to be full-on combat against a well-prepared, heavily entrenched, and committed enemy. I expected high casualties from intense urban combat, with civilian deaths and subsequent enemy propaganda coups in the media.

Al Qaeda does not rely on force strength. When attacked in large numbers, they fight for a while and then try to escape or blend in with the locals. So the bridges across the Diyala River, which splits the city of Baqubah down the middle, would have to be controlled. The neighborhoods would have to be cordoned off and then carefully and deliberately cleared. Meanwhile, al Qaeda was expecting an attack and had rigged the city with IEDs and booby-trapped houses. I would later hear General Petraeus say that Baqubah had been the most "rigged city" of the entire war. More so even than Fallujah, where the Coalition had suffered serious losses.

The first full day of Operation Arrowhead Ripper on June 20 was intense. The army gave me full access to the battlefield and the Tactical Operations Command (TOC). I saw the raw truth on the ground and as it fed through the various communication and observation technologies in TOC. Apart from special operations, they hid nothing. A reporter was able to see as much as he or she could stand.

The heat on that first day was blistering, for the enemy and for us. Any chance they got, combat soldiers would lie down during the heat of day, in complete body armor and helmets, and fall asleep in the dirt. Our guys were tough. The enemy in Baqubah was as good as any in Iraq, and better than most. That was saying a lot. But our guys systematically cornered them, and foiled some big traps the enemy had set.

By the end of the first day, about thirty enemy had been killed, one U.S. soldier was killed, and five were wounded in action. At least two soldiers were heat casualties, including one who was with my group.

One positive indicator was how the locals reacted. Beginning that first day, civilians in Baqubah pointed out IEDs and hidden enemy fighters to our troops.

For security reasons, the Iraq Army had not been included in the initial planning of Arrowhead Ripper. Yet with each succeeding day they took a larger role in the unfolding attack. The 5th Iraqi Army Division was an increasingly competent group of fighters. The 5th was committed to battle. The local police force was less impressive.

I spent June 22 (D-Day plus 3) with the 3-2 Stryker Brigade Combat Team. I had run a few missions with them in Baghdad, and they had fought all over Iraq. The Brigade had much recent combat experience and was expertly commanded. One did not need to meet the commanders (though I did each day) to know they were running a tight ship.

The combat in Baqubah was about to reach a peak. Al Qaeda seemed to have been effectively isolated. Despite security leaks, the timing of the initial attack on June 19 achieved enough surprise that many al Qaeda were caught off guard and trapped. They had been beaten back mostly into pockets and were surrounded. Part of this was due to the capability of Strykers and the new fighting doctrines used by Stryker Brigades, which made it possible for even a large force to "attack from the march" with great agility. The Strykers driving in from Baghdad and elsewhere quickly locked down Baqubah, while other attacking forces came by helicopters. Because of the security leaks, some of the leadership is believed to have escaped. But the capture of at least one possible high-value target in Baqubah, and seven men who were caught trying to escape while dressed as women, indicated that not all al Qaeda leaders successfully fled in advance of the battle.

On the battlefield, our guys were winning street by street. And an increasing number of Iraqis were turning to our side and bringing intelligence about where enemy assets were stashed or lying in wait. Former enemies, such as members of the 1920 Revolution Brigades, rode alongside us into combat, and were doing all manner of tricks against the enemy. American soldiers called them "Kit Carson Scouts." The scouts, and the information they delivered, might have been worth another ten thousand Americans. They were devastating for al Qaeda and invaluable for us in circumventing ambushes. And the only reason they were riding with us instead of al Qaeda was that we controlled the moral high ground. (An insurgent leader and former avowed enemy of the Americans named Abu Ali told me the 1920s in Baqubah turned against AQI in Baqubah in early April 2007 because of AQI crimes. The 1920s reached out to the Coalition just days later.) It's probably accurate to say that our former avowed enemies saved us dozens of fatalities during the first days. Some of the tricks employed by the Kit Carson Scouts were very clever and took great courage, but this is no time to write about them; the war is not over yet, and we still need those tricks.

★　　★　　★

As those first several days merged into a blur, the fate of al Qaeda was clear: they were about to be strangled and pummeled to death in Baqubah. But also clear from the first day was how deficient the local city government had become. I grasped the challenge watching the local leadership fumble the problem of several hundred IDP (Internally Displaced Persons) in the city.

These were mostly moms and kids, who needed to be fed and otherwise taken care of. LTC Fred Johnson, deputy commanding officer of 3rd Stryker Brigade Combat Team, 2nd Infantry Division (3-2 SBCT), actually took me out to see them himself. I had been with LTC Fred Johnson for several days. He seemed to recharge on sunlight or moonlight and could run a man into the ground. When we arrived to see the IDPs, the kids looked happy and wanted their photos taken, but the moms looked worried. Seeing that inept local Iraqi leaders were doing little to avert what soon would be a crisis, LTC Johnson started jerking choke chains on the people who were supposed to be handling humanitarian needs. Over the course of a few days, I had seen these same Iraqis in meeting after meeting, finding ways to be underachievers. The Iraqi commanders had dozens of large trucks. They had only to drive to our base to collect the supplies and distribute them to the people displaced by the battle. Our troops were fully engaged in combat, yet the Iraqi leaders were not able to organize a few trucks without LTC Johnson supplying the initiative. The Kurds would have already fixed this problem. Likewise, the Iraqi commanders in Mosul or Hit.

In the city, Iraqi locals kept telling me, "Thank you, Thank you." They were saying this much more often than I'd heard it before. The young women would surreptitiously flirt with American soldiers, waving and smiling at them. They kept their hands very close to their bodies so others could not see them waving, or even occasionally blowing kisses at soldiers.

Planning the Battle with the Peace in Mind

In the early days of the battle, Colonel Steve Townsend, the respected 3-2 Stryker brigade commander, reported that at least fifty enemy had been killed. Townsend always seemed to be conservative, while his subordinate commanders put the number as high as one hundred. More than sixty suspects were in custody, but Townsend was unsure how many of the suspects were truly AQI. American losses by now included one soldier killed in action, with twenty-one wounded. One Bradley and one Stryker had been destroyed. One reason we took so few casualties was that the clearing operation was slow and methodical; success was not measured against the clock. In meeting after meeting, I saw Townsend stress to his subordinate commanders the importance of moving deliberately and at their own pace. Given the massive amounts of IEDs that were found, we might have taken dozens more killed if the clearing operation had been rushed.

There were more than two-dozen houses and buildings rigged as giant bombs, and civilians pointed out many of those. Our soldiers and Iraqi soldiers simply stopped, cleared out the people, and then destroyed the buildings, but each time they worked harder to mitigate damage to surrounding houses. They were planning for the day after the fighting stopped when they would need the people's trust and good will, so for this battle they came prepared to compensate people for unavoidable damages when they occurred.

We also had some luck. Soldiers entered a home filled with explosives, but somehow escaped without injury. There were some extremely close calls by IEDs that could have been catastrophic to soldiers, but led to only ringing ears and sore bodies. Sometimes the escapes resulted from pure luck, while other times the escapes were more attributable to combat experienced 3-2 soldiers who were keenly on their game, who escaped bombs that likely would have killed rookies.

The air force made the clearing operation safer by dropping bombs on some of the rigged homes. MLRS missiles were fired into others. Townsend's soldiers returned to an area they had just cleared. The squad leader spotted a vegetable can that had not been there minutes earlier. But it was too late: the vegetable can blew up, the squad went down from the blast, and the enemy started shooting. Six soldiers were wounded then, but expected to return to duty. Incidents like this were so commonplace that they were only noteworthy if you were the one hit.

Bird's Eye View

About 3:00 A.M. on June 23, a jet roared low and loud over the tents. Some soldiers rolled out of their cots to the floor, thinking it was "incoming." I lay there in the tent looking into the darkness. The night quieted. Then I heard a Shadow launch from its catapult somewhere in the distance, sounding like a weed-eater as it flew into the darkness. Something was up. I couldn't sleep, so I rolled out of bed and pulled on my boots and headed over to the TOC.

A Tactical Operations Center (TOC) is the headquarters for a unit, packed with communications and monitoring equipment, radios, and video screens. The radios are for communication between the different companies, as well as helicopters and jets. Battalion-level TOCs also communicate laterally with other battalions and vertically up to the brigade. Usually some ten soldiers will sit in front of the screens. One soldier will be the S-2, or intelligence. Another will monitor counter-battery radar. Another will communicate with those who operate the unmanned aerial vehicle (UAV), which often is launched and controlled from elsewhere. A battalion can "task" the UAV, but an outside unit actually maintains, launches, and flies it. In Baqubah, Shadows—unarmed UAVs—were launched from their catapults or buzzing overhead every day that weather permitted.

I entered the TOC about 3:20 A.M., and there was a video feed coming in from an F-16. Crosshairs were steady on a house the pilot was circling. We could sometimes hear the jet as it passed overhead during the orbit. The Shadow was circling the same house but from a lower altitude, and both feeds were streaming live.

"What's up with the house?" I asked.

"An element took SAFIRE [small-arms fire] and the enemy ran into that house."

"What're you gonna do?"

"Trying to decide. Probably bomb it."

Sounds simple. Question is, bomb it with what? The commanders had myriad options. Some weapons were within their direct authority to use, while other weapons required higher permission. Rules of Engagement (ROE) changed constantly. For the early days of Operation Arrowhead Ripper, the ROE were relaxed, giving robust options further down the chain, with the caveat to mitigate civilian deaths. In all, there were seven known civilian fatalities. A number that low—and five of those deaths were from a single explosion that locals said had come from a U.S. bomb—is almost unbelievable, considering the amount of firepower that had been used. Our commanders made avoiding civilian casualties a primary part of the battle plan.

With the enemy hiding in the building, an F–16 and a Shadow orbiting above, and both peering down on thermal mode, the battle captain asked the air force experts (the JTACs or Joint Tactical Air Controllers) what weapons the F–16 was carrying. The jets carried a mixture of weapons cross-loaded between them, in order to have the right tool needed for any given situation. To use just the proportionate amount of force to kill the enemy fighters, but leave everyone in the surrounding area unscathed, if possible. Now was option time. Which weapon to use? There were many choices: mortars, missiles, cannons of various sorts, among others. By about 0400 (4 A.M.), the battle captain had decided to use 120mm mortars, substantial enough to obliterate a car, but not a two-story house made of concrete. The first mortar round was fired, and black-hot thermal clouds on the two video screens showed it hit hundreds of yards off target. Successive shots were only worse. It was starting to look like a turkey shoot, so the battle captain ordered the mortars to cease fire.

They discussed dropping a JDAM (Joint Direct Attack Munition) from one of the jets. A JDAM is a smart bomb with a GPS-based guidance system. But a JDAM might cause too much collateral damage. The idea of a strafe run came up, but that would likely cause even more collateral damage, so that was also nixed. The F-16 was carrying at least one concrete bomb—literally just a bomb made from concrete, like throwing boulders at people— but a JTAC said, "We are not dropping a concrete bomb." For some reason he didn't want to just throw a rock. But a strange feeling came over me: I wanted to see the F-16 drop a boulder on the people that shot at our guys. Also I knew if the rock hit the bad guys, the neighbors would be fine.

While the TOC crew and the air force guys were discussing how best to kill the enemy, the F-16 was running low on fuel. So in the end the jets just flew low in a show of force and then rumbled away.

I walked to breakfast while they were still plotting their next move. I have no idea if they killed the enemy and if they did what method they finally settled on. But I know that there was careful deliberation in the TOC, combined with excellent combat soldiers on the streets. That was how civilian casualties, as well as our own losses, were kept so astonishingly low.

I wrote my first dispatches during Operation Arrowhead Ripper with explosions, gunfire, and the sounds of helicopters and jets in the background. After a few days the fighting decreased remarkably, but the last pockets still held enemy and bombs.

Nobody yet knew what awaited the soldiers as they cleared Baqubah inch by inch, street by street, but day by day our folks were gaining the high ground in the flat city of Baqubah.

CHAPTER ELEVEN

Al Qaeda on the Run

On June 29, American and Iraqi soldiers were again fighting side by side. Soldiers from Charley Company 1-12 CAV—led by Captain Clayton Combs—and Iraqi soldiers from the 5th IA, closed in on a village on the outskirts of Baqubah. CPT Combs has been fighting hard in Diyala for about ten months, often working with the Iraqi 5th Division. Most of the American officers and sergeants who work with the 5th have good things to report about them, and Combs is no exception. He tells me this particular Iraqi unit, the 3-25, has never run away from combat and never refused to close on the enemy. "They have always come when I am in trouble," Combs said. "They always go on patrols when I ask. They never back down."

The village we were closing on had the misfortune of being located near a main road—about three and a half miles from FOB Warhorse—that al Qaeda liked to bomb. Al Qaeda had taken over the village. As Iraqi and American soldiers moved in, they came under light contact, but the bombs planted in the roads (and maybe in the houses) were the real threat. One by one, demolition experts destroyed the bombs, leaving craters in the unpaved roads.

But when our soldiers entered the village they found it abandoned. All the people were gone. But where?

The next day, soldiers from 1-12 CAV allowed me to go to the village in one of their M-1 tanks. When we arrived at the outskirts, American soldiers began unloading dozens of body bags, which the grim-faced Iraqi soldiers carried into the village.

As we continued on through the village, CPT Combs pointed out the nice houses, saying the people had been simple farmers with comfortable homes and lives.

Until al Qaeda showed up.

Now the houses were all empty. We walked by two donkeys, each shot in the neck. Al Qaeda had killed the people's livestock. They often hide bombs inside dead animals or dead people. We passed by a crater—one of many in the village—made the day before when bomb experts destroyed an IED. Just beyond the crater, CPT Combs pointed out a car that had been filled with explosives. American soldiers had destroyed it with a Thermite grenade.

As we passed more abandoned homes, I saw an empty AK-47 magazine on the ground. The houses were in shambles; broken glass and ski masks littered the area.

We walked into the palm groves nearby. There was a terrible stench. The heat and the vegetation reminded me of the Killing Fields in Cambodia where I had visited before returning to Iraq.

Soldiers from 5th IA said they'd found some of the villagers— dead. Iraqi soldiers were excavating several graves. The bodies were fresh, and the smell was overwhelming. A small group of American soldiers were keeping a respectful distance, but the area was filled with Iraqi soldiers from 5th IA.

I told the Iraqi commander, Captain Baker, that it was important that Americans see this. He took me to the graves and showed me more than I wanted to see. He said these people had been murdered by al Qaeda. The heat was crushing, about 115° F and humid. The overpowering stench of decaying human flesh made my stomach feel like it was being punched. The only sounds were shovels striking earth as Iraqi soldiers kept digging.

There were bodies of men, women, and children. There was no sign of the sacred at this gravesite. The corpses were stashed in shallow graves. In one grave, soldiers recovered the heads of decapitated children, some with still partially recognizable remnants of flesh and hair. Some of the bodies seemed fresh, while others had been there longer.

By the time I arrived, the Iraqi soldiers had uncovered parts of six bodies. From what I could see, they did not all appear to have been murdered at once. In one grave, there were exposed ribs and other bones, although there was still flesh on the bones.

The digging was the first part of the gruesome job. It was hot, hard work. As it progressed, the stench got worse and worse. An Iraqi soldier carefully sprinkled water on the corpses.

The Iraqi soldiers were barely talking. All had grim looks and everybody seemed to want to be a million miles away. Iraqi soldiers said that al Qaeda had cut the heads off the children. Had al Qaeda murdered the children in front of their parents? It could have been the other way around—they might have murdered the parents in front of the children. Or maybe they had forced fathers to dig the graves of their children.

Later that day, some of the soldiers from the unit I share a tent with, the C–52, told me that when one of their Iraqi Kit Carson Scouts spotted a man he claimed was an al Qaeda terrorist who had cut off the heads of children, the scout freaked out and tried to hide. The soldiers of C–52 took the suspected al Qaeda to the police. The Iraqi Police knew the man and reacted furiously. One, crazed with anger, drew his pistol to shoot the man and had to be restrained. The soldiers told me it took almost forty-five minutes to calm him down; then he got angry again when an American soldier gave the al Qaeda man a drink of cold water.

While that was happening elsewhere in Baqubah, we stood around the stinking graves of people who had gotten a close-up view of al Qaeda-style justice. The bodies were rotting in the heat before us.

The blade of the shovel struck more fingers, and the Iraqi soldiers stopped and pointed to the fingers so I could film them. But I had seen enough and pulled back into the palm groves.

The Enemy of My Enemy

Al Qaeda's No. 2 asks support of Muslims
Lee Keath, Associated Press Writer
Baghdad, July 5, 2007

Al-Qaeda's deputy leader sought to bolster the terror network's main arm in Iraq in a new video released Thursday, calling on Muslims to rally behind it at a time when the group is on the defensive, faced with U.S. offensives and splits with other insurgent groups.

Several large Iraqi insurgent groups publicly denounced al Qaeda, saying its fighters were killing theirs and pressuring them to join the Islamic state. One group, the 1920 Revolution Brigades, has begun overtly cooperating with U.S. forces and Sunni tribal leaders to attack al Qaeda.

In early 2005, I had accompanied a mission in Baqubah into a then fantastically dangerous neighborhood called Buhriz. One of the groups making it so dangerous was the 1920 Revolution

Brigades, a very tough, proficient group of Sunni fighters. Had we been faced with a combined force of 1920s and al Qaeda in Baqubah in June 2007, Operation Arrowhead Ripper likely would have been a much bloodier battle for our side. That didn't happen because in April the 1920s had reached out to American soldiers, and together they began dismantling al Qaeda.

In early July 2007, I found myself back on the streets of Buhriz talking with Abu Ali, a leading member of the 1920s. Just months ago our forces would have shot Abu Ali on sight, and he likely would have shot us.

I asked Abu Ali why he and the 1920s turned against al Qaeda. He was direct and clear in his speech, and his soft-spoken manner was similar to that of many experienced American combat leaders. Abu Ali said: "Al Qaeda is an abomination of Islam: cutting off heads, stealing people's money, kidnapping, and every type of torture."

One Iraqi official had described to me the way al Qaeda had infiltrated Diyala province. When al Qaeda came to Baqubah, they first united many of the otherwise independent criminal gangs. They recruited boys between the ages of fourteen and sixteen and gave them weapons, including pistols, a bicycle, a cell phone (with phone cards paid) and a salary of $100 per month. These boys were used for kidnapping, torture, and murder.

At first, the official had said they would only target Shia (thus stoking civil war and provoking the growth of Shia militias, who would become extremely deadly to Sunni and to us), but over time al Qaeda directed attacks against anyone who thought differently than they did, including Sunni. Apparently most of the estimated one thousand al Qaeda fighters in Baqubah were young men and boys who called the city home. Al Qaeda had relied heavily on local talent, made easier to recruit because of the civil war al Qaeda had fomented. When the locals turned against al Qaeda, the organization was doomed.

Iraqis love and greatly value their children. This makes children especially vulnerable as targets for terrorists. That is a brutal fact. The official had gone on to say that on a couple of occasions in Baqubah, al Qaeda invited to lunch families they wanted to convert to their way of thinking. In each instance the family had a boy about eleven years old. When the families sat down to eat, their boy was brought in with his mouth stuffed. The boy had been baked. Al Qaeda served the boy to his family. My repeated attempts to verify the story failed to produce concrete proof, although many had heard similar stories. But the rumors showed how terrible al Qaeda's reputation for atrocities had become among the local people.

Ali told me people had been afraid in their own homes because of al Qaeda. And so Abu Ali and the local 1920s were the latest al Qaeda paradox. Al Qaeda, which nearly ripped Iraq apart, was driving former enemies into what I believe could be long-term alliances with U.S. forces. The 1920s knew that our people had moral fiber and were completely unafraid to close with al Qaeda and were eager to engage al Qaeda in combat at any chance. The 1920s had come to respect U.S. forces for the punishment and losses U.S. soldiers could take, yet still keep clobbering 1920s, al Qaeda, and JAM, all at the same time. That respect helped create common ground. We all knew that we had to destroy al Qaeda.

Al Qaeda had made the 1920s in Baqubah our ally.

I asked Abu Ali if he had fought Americans and Ali laughed. "What kind of question is that?" he replied, which made me chuckle. I asked if there was something he would like to say to the Americans. After thinking for a moment, he said, "I ask one thing: After the Iraqi Army and Police Service take hold and the security forces are ready, we want a schedule for the American forces to leave." It was not said with hostility, but Ali did not want his country governed by any foreign occupiers.

As Ali went off with another American unit, the rest of us loaded back into the Stryker and drove past bustling markets that had been closed under al Qaeda. The Iraqis smiled and waved at us in the same streets where only recently we had been killing each other. Within weeks of the battle, life was already beginning to improve for the Iraqis of Baqubah.

On July 7, General Petraeus visited the city, but there was near-zero fuss, and the day wasn't much different from any other. Petraeus had lunch with commanders, followed by a series of briefings the press was allowed to attend. After the briefings, Petraeus headed downtown to an area where many of the buildings had been made into bombs.

At the beginning of Operation Arrowhead Ripper, I thought dozens of soldiers might be killed and hundreds wounded. The terrorists had done a much more thorough job rigging Baqubah with explosive traps than they had in either Fallujah or Ramadi prior to Coalition assaults. During one of General Petraeus's briefings that Saturday, he mentioned that Baqubah was probably the most rigged city of the entire war. One officer said there was so much explosives residue in Baqubah that the bomb dogs were getting confused. But street by street, house by house, step by step, infantry soldiers cleared most of Baqubah. Troops found more than one hundred thirty bombs planted in ambush, about two dozen buildings rigged to explode, and more than half a dozen car bombs. The people pointed out most of the ambushes.

Temperatures rose to 120° F during the day. Some soldiers went more than ten days without a shower, wearing heavy gear and sleeping in baked-on filth. The one thing the heat did not do was keep them awake. Soldiers this tired will sleep on hot, broken glass on the ground outside a blown-up building.

And as the soldiers cleared Baqubah of the enemy and its deadly traps, the people came forward and talked. They were happy to be liberated, and this truly was a liberation. Other than in the Kurdish areas, I had never seen such overt gratitude from so many Iraqis directed to American soldiers.

While the methodical clearing of Baqubah's neighborhoods continued, and the local Iraqis continued to point out al Qaeda operatives and hidden bombs, the Islamic State of Iraq, the public face of al Qaeda's franchise in Baqubah, issued a statement to the press. It was reminiscent of the interviews Baghdad Bob used to give in the days immediately following the invasion in 2003, explaining how there was not a single American soldier in Baghdad as our armor was rolling through the streets.

"The strongest kinds of explosives are awaiting them on the streets and in the alleys. Snipers of the Islamic State of Iraq are going ahead hunting down dozens of soldiers. They are in control of the high-rise buildings, and ambushes and traps are awaiting them everywhere. The American Army, in spite of its numbers and equipment, could not penetrate the region except for a couple of minutes to film so as to sell the photographs to the lying media. [Nobody is happy with the media, it seems.] It is during those few minutes that a great number of airplanes were downed. We are announcing this good news to the nation, as the soldiers of the Islamic State of Iraq are basking in their victory in all parts of this and the rest of the provinces, while the Crusaders will not escape this fierce battle but with slit throats and a defeat, the likes of which has never been witnessed."

Whatever the effect of this propaganda on the world at large, the people of Baqubah were laughing and smoking cigarettes, and al Qaeda was running scared. They had been evicted from Anbar and most of Baghdad, and now Baqubah and many other places were becoming hostile territory. Running out of places to go, they mostly headed further out into Diyala province and up to Salah ad Din, Kirkuk, and Nineveh provinces (where Mosul was guarded by the 2-7 CAV) with our folks and the Iraqi Army in hot pursuit, but not too hot. Some commanders wanted to stay on al Qaeda's heels, but we didn't have enough troops for that, and we had already learned that chasing al Qaeda without truly securing what we just fought for was a sure way to lose it again.

Al Qaeda's values in action had, yet again, lost them the people. Al Qaeda has a losing formula, like a crack habit. And we were actually starting to beat them not just on the battlefield but in the media: now it was al Qaeda whining about the "lying media." Our military had morphed before my eyes into savvy fighters for the media battle space. And although some PAOs (Public Affairs Offices) continued to give me personal grief, most were doing excellent work and were getting their side of the story out. More and more newspapers reported accurately from the field. Conservative readers were still giving the *New York Times* grief, but I saw Michael Gordon and Rich Oppel working tirelessly, reporting the news accurately and not reflexively straining for a negative note to end any positive news item. Alexandra Zavis from the *LA Times* was another reporter working hard and getting it right. And though the AP sullied its name in Iraq and became a casualty of this war, there were good folks at AP such as Maya Alleruzzo and Talal Mohammed, the Iraqi stringer I had done a number of missions within Baqubah.

On July 28, 2007, Talal and a friend were kidnapped near Baqubah. Talal was never seen again. When his friend was released, he reported that they were taken to a farm and kept apart, but he could hear Talal being beaten and interrogated in the next room. I have heard estimates that of the more than one hundred twenty-five journalists killed by the end of 2004, more than one hundred were Iraqi. Sources vary as to the exact numbers, but all agree that this is the most dangerous war in history for journalists, and Iraqis have gotten the worst of it by far.

In my experience, U.S. forces treat Iraqi journalists, such as Talal Mohammed, like honored guests. I'd seen Lieutenant Colonel Fred Johnson invite Talal on missions, and especially to meetings, because Johnson wanted Talal to tell people what he was seeing. In just a few short months, I'd seen how unit after unit was opening its doors and accommodating media, welcoming them in fact. (Though even in 2008, there do remain "media challenged" commanders and units.) This was a primary reason that we started destroying al Qaeda in the media. We had truth on our side, and our folks were mostly open—with obvious limits where security demanded. Over time this worked in our favor. Despite plenty of negative stories, the net effect has been increasingly accurate press, and not a moment too soon. Accurate press benefits the U.S. military.

The killing, scattering, and capturing of al Qaeda was only part of the fight. During the invasion in 2003, the Coalition did the same to Saddam's army, and then watched Iraq fall apart. Yet in Baqubah there was a "full-spectrum" operation where the perceptions of local people were of primary importance. And the push was on to make the kind of substantive changes in the quality of people's lives that could withstand mere propaganda any day.

CHAPTER TWELVE

Walking Tall:
Tonto and The Mayor

Operation Arrowhead Ripper went down like a gigantic raid, like a tiger pouncing, though prior security leaks allowed many al Qaeda leaders to flee ahead of our advancing troops. Most of those who remained were killed or captured, often fingered by the locals who had previously supported them. But for LTC Fred Johnson, deputy commanding officer of the 3rd Stryker Brigade Combat Team, 2nd Infantry Division (3-2 SBCT), the raid was just the beginning of the counterinsurgency. After vanquishing al Qaeda, U.S. forces could not afford to lose momentum as had happened so many times before, so the plan was to have no pause before the restoration of services. Lessons that Petraeus demonstrated in Mosul in 2003 were directly applied in Baqubah in June–July of 2007. Johnson and other commanders pushed to get local leaders to take responsibility for running the local government as soon as possible, even while the guns were still firing. Equal parts soldier, diplomat, coach, and judge, all strapped to a high-performance engine, Johnson was the man for the first big job.

Warrior Statesmen

While Operation Arrowhead Ripper was still a kinetic and contested battle, commanders kept popping out of combat to attend meetings for local civil affairs projects. The commanders would come in sweating and dirty, then switch gears to talk diplomatically—and sometimes not so diplomatically—about electricity, fuel, water and food distribution. They came in after having been in firefights the very same hour, and sat down to talk politics, and then went out and kept fighting al Qaeda. They alternated between teatime, firefight, teatime again, while figuring out food distribution, firefight, raid, IED, collapse from exhaustion, firefight, teatime, while arguing about some water pipes and then firefight again. It's hard to forget people like LTC Avanulas Smiley and Morris "Mo" Goins. They seemed to have been made for this type of extreme physical and mental agility.

This agility was transmitted down through the ranks. Young soldiers were learning huge lessons that would never be taught in school. They had to be able to fight hard yet switch gears from the brutality and stresses of combat nearly instantly back to the "real world," though nearly all had learned that combat was more "real" and immediate than anything they had ever seen. They were applying those lessons at their level, by mentoring Iraqi Police and Army. The 5th Iraqi Army division was fighting hard, side-by-side, and doing better than I had seen the Iraq Army do before.

This job of kick-starting the government fell on the shoulders of the American commanders because most of the experienced local leaders were either living abroad or had been victims of al Qaeda. The new leaders had little experience, or lacked the natural instinct to solve the many problems their city faced. So our soldiers mentored Iraqi civil leaders. In meeting after meeting,

American military leaders revealed an important yet hidden collective skill set: they know how to run a city.

How is it that a group of commanders seem to understand how to run a city? Because they do it all the time, even at home.

The American military governs city-states—bases—all over the world. A commander who runs an American military base in Iraq is referred to as the "Mayor," and he or she must understand the vital functions of a city and how it operates. This includes water, electricity, sewage, food distribution, police, courts, prisons, hospitals, fire, schools, airports, ports, trash control, vector control, communications, fuel, and fiscal budgeting, for example. Base commanders in the U.S. must deal with local political leaders; base commanders abroad must be international diplomats.

American troops lived far better on base than many of the people who lived in downtown Baqubah (although there were some very nice homes). And when Americans moved into Iraqi buildings, those buildings started improving from the first day. Soon the buildings nearby began to improve.

It was not about the money. It was about the mindset, the "can-do mentality." The belief that problems are to be solved, by us, now. When I listened to Iraqis in civil affairs meetings inventorying the obstacles, giving detailed and passionate speeches about why certain goals were impossible, I often heard a tired lament. "You can do these things because America is rich. You put a man on the moon!" Which made me think, "I know a 22-year-old buck sergeant who never went to college and who's guarding the door who could figure out a lot of these problems if his commander told him to."

Part of Johnson's challenge was simply convincing the Iraqis that obstacles could be overcome and problems solved, demonstrating that our material advantages were the result not the cause of our abilities and character. Every time Johnson and his soldiers heard an Iraqi government official exclaim, "It *can't* be done!" they had to reply with deeds as well as words, so the combined response was not just "Yes, it *can!*" but also "and here's how."

Iraqis weren't alone in their pessimism. Many voices back home in America were saying that the problems facing Iraq demanded political, not military, solutions. Our forces could win battles, the naysayers reasoned, and it wouldn't matter because the political solutions were not happening. But politics—smart politics—was *exactly* what Fred Johnson and other soldiers from the 3-2 SBCT were doing in Baqubah. With Petraeus at the helm, American commanders all across Iraq were conducting classic and brilliant counterinsurgency, which meant they were forging political change. During 2007, as I traveled around Iraq, it became increasingly rare to stumble upon an American commander acting like the monkey in the cockpit pushing the red buttons. Based on what I saw from that summer on in Iraq, I increasingly came to believe that most of this war could be ended through smart politics and that commanders like Fred Johnson could make it happen.

Bread and a Circus

The best politician often leaves no traces of his handiwork. To make a solution stick, the local parties must be able to claim responsibility, even to the extent of believing they did it themselves. To pull that off requires, even under the best of conditions, adroit leadership. These were not the best of conditions. Bringing people together to solve problems requires compromise. But in a nation like Iraq in the midst of a civil war (even if now rapidly winding down), compromise can be taken as a sign of weakness. Weakness can get people killed in Iraq.

At the beginning of Operation Arrowhead Ripper, the city of Baqubah had not had a food shipment for ten months. Iraq uses a voucher-based food distribution system that predates the invasion and hearkens back to the sanctions and trade restrictions Iraqis had to live with because of Saddam's transgressions against the world. Basically, there is one "food agent" for about every two hundred families, and those families get vouchers to pick up food from local warehouses. Each family receives a stipend from the Iraqi government, and some of that money is automatically deducted for food. When the shipments of food from Baghdad were halted, it meant that the people of Baqubah had been paying for food for ten months but not getting the food. People weren't starving in Baqubah. But that did not keep them from being angry that food shipments for which they'd already paid were being held up in Baghdad.

Al Qaeda used food for clout and for pocket money. When al Qaeda seized the food warehouse in Baqubah, the authorities in Baghdad responded by cutting off food shipments to Baqubah. This served al Qaeda's purposes well because it meant they had effectively cleaved Baqubah off from Baghdad. The mostly Shiite government in Baghdad became the bad guys for cutting off the food: the Baghdad food warehouse is at Sadr City: Shiite-land. Meanwhile, in the eyes of the people in Baghdad who controlled the food distribution, Baqubah was a Ba'athist haven and al Qaeda headquarters. Al Qaeda had picked its shots well.

The battle plan included not just destroying or flushing al Qaeda but convincing the people of Baqubah that life would improve immediately. Getting the food distribution going again would be evidence of that and it was also low-hanging fruit. There was an abundance of problems that would take time, but to get the food shipments moving again, all we had to do was get trucks safely down to Baghdad and back to Baqubah. The food was in Baghdad. It was a stationary target. Simple.

Or so it seemed.

The meetings between American officers and Iraqi officials in Baqubah were long and frustrating, with the Iraqis putting far more energy into explaining why food distribution would not work than in finding ways to make it work.

Not that all the problems were imaginary. The Mayor of Baqubah and his subordinates were justifiably afraid to go near Sadr City to get that food from the warehouse. The Mayor told me that when another government representative from Baqubah went to another warehouse to get medical supplies, he disappeared. The Mayor told me flat out that if he went to the food warehouse, he would be killed.

LTC Johnson was convinced he had to get the food distribution going both to build credibility with the people of Baqubah and help the frightened and demoralized local civil leadership get a success under their belts. He would get them to mount a convoy from Baqubah to Baghdad, to meet with Ministry of Trade officials (who handled food distribution) and get the food.

Johnson brought along an Iraqi journalist; food distribution was a critical battle, and he wanted that victory celebrated and accentuated in the Iraqi media. Most of the Western press had missed the initial fight in Baqubah, because they had not known it was coming. Then when they saw it was an overwhelming victory for our side, most of them left immediately. What they didn't get was that the real story was just beginning to unfold. It was no big news that we could blow al Qaeda out of a town, though doing it with so few casualties was more than notable. The big story would be the restoration of a functioning civil order, with Iraqis in charge, in the immediate aftermath of a civil war, in a country that had been run by a brutal centralized dictatorship for decades. The 3-2 Stryker Battalion Combat Team are a smart and experienced lot. They made no pretension of hiding their motivations for inviting me: they knew I was apt to stay around even if there was no fighting.

Johnson's convoy problems began as soon as the trucks lined up that morning in Baqubah. Apache helicopters patrolled overhead as Major Kenneth Daniels sat down to talk with truck drivers, soldiers, and government officials. The truckers had agreed to go to Baghdad to pick up the food only because Americans were going to escort them. They said they knew Americans would not leave them if something happened. About half the trucks were ready to go, but needed fuel, so Fred Johnson called another American unit at Forward Operating Base (FOB) Warhorse. The re-fuelers had no idea about the problem, but loaded up and brought two trucks of fuel into Baqubah. This was a trivial issue for American forces to solve, but would have been a show-stopper for Iraqis. Once the fuel problem was solved, the convoy headed toward Baghdad.

Can you believe I nearly shot him?

On the way to Baghdad, the Iraqi civilian convoy diverted to a quicker route. The dangerous shortcut caused them to arrive an hour before we did. The break in contact led to frustrating hours of additional delay as we tooled around Baghdad trying to find the warehouse and then re-establishing contact with all the trucks. Meanwhile, we had to stop several times, dismounting into the scorching heat so the Mayor could make calls on his cell phone. Each time we dismounted, Staff Sergeant Matt Hudgeons's job was to counter-snipe; snipers were a serious threat.

With all the delays, by the time we arrived, the Ministry and the food warehouse near Sadr City were closed. (Civil servants leave at 2 P.M.) This was more than an inconvenience. The drivers were afraid to stay overnight in Baghdad. Yet if they went home to Baqubah driving empty trucks, the food mission would likely crash. The Iraqi media were watching. If the drivers left, the mission would not only fail, it would backfire, sending the message that even with al Qaeda being toppled in Baqubah, Baqubah was still abandoned by the Iraqi government in Baghdad. This would be a terrific media victory for al Qaeda.

Some drivers wanted desperately to go home. The Mayor was having second thoughts: he seemed, if anything, more frightened than the drivers, which undermined the drivers' morale. Then the Iraqi soldiers who had been part of the convoy announced they were heading back to Baqubah for the night. They promised to be back at 6:00 A.M. the next morning, which of course we all doubted. The mission was dissolving into futility.

LTC Johnson bristled as he spoke to the collapsing convoy. In clear and commanding tones, he told the Iraqi men that that the future of their country depended on moments like this, happening right then all over Iraq, where men either stood their ground or ran away and gave the day to the terrorists. Johnson's words carried particular weight because of an encounter earlier that day.

That morning, while we were still trying to get the convoy organized, an Iraqi had approached with something that looked like intent in his eyes. Johnson closed on the man, whom he suspected was a suicide bomber. Johnson drew his pistol. If a bomb had detonated, Johnson and a few others definitely would have been killed. I might have survived, but solely because Johnson and the others had closed space with the man. They risked their lives not to save mine but the suspected bomber's. They could have shot the man from a distance; instead they moved straight toward him. That was courage. Everyone saw it. I photographed it.

As it happened, the man was coming to help start the convoy rolling. The man—I'll call him "Tonto" for his own safety—owned some trucks and wanted to get his business going. Tonto wanted in on the convoy. Guts and capitalism make an impressive combination.

That afternoon in Baghdad, when the Iraqi truck drivers and the Mayor were ready to turn tail, Tonto seized the moment. Tonto told Johnson he had about ten drivers who agreed to stay. Johnson began to focus on Tonto, a man he had nearly shot hours earlier. Johnson turned to the Mayor and told him to load up with the other cowards and go home to Baqubah. He actually called them cowards. For this mission to work, he said, the people of Baqubah needed men with guts to carry it off, so Johnson would work through the logistics with Tonto, all one hundred twenty pounds of him. There was some arguing and shouting among the truckers, and somewhere the Mayor caught a little courage. Within minutes the other Iraqis bucked up and decided to stay. Tonto had made the difference—and as it turned out not for the last time. In the weeks ahead, Johnson would say to me more than once, "Can you believe I nearly shot him?"

There was good reason for the truckers to be afraid and Johnson wanted to stay and guard them. But the garage owners where the trucks were parked did not want Americans staying overnight, so we headed to Camp Liberty in Baghdad. Johnson asked the Mayor if he wanted to come, and after some thought, he did.

This was tricky stuff Johnson was trying to pull off. He was keeping the prestige of the Mayor intact by taking him with us. There would be a night to shore up his courage, and Johnson needed the Mayor to demonstrate courage in the morning in front of his people. Then the Iraqi facility for turning rumor into legend could turn the Mayor into the Lion of Baqubah, and Baqubah needed some lions.

The next morning we loaded into the Strykers long before sunrise and drove off base into the dangerous streets of Baghdad. Before 6:00 A.M., we had avoided IEDs, EFPs, and whatever else might have been set to kill us and were back at the parking lot where we met up with all the drivers. Tonto had stayed with his men and machines. I expected we might find them decapitated and maybe with explosives stuffed in their bellies. They weren't. But they did look happy to see us.

And then the 5th IA arrived. On time. With all the right gear. Ready for work. God is great.

Escorting the trucks was dangerous. Snipers, EFPs, suicide car bombs—the whole party could be and would be out there waiting for us. We made it to the Ministry where the bureaucrats, who were all Shiites, were about to be confronted by the Sunni Mayor of Baqubah.

Sunni and Shia get along well in many places. There are mixed neighborhoods and mixed families. Iraqi military units are often mixed and work well together. But here was a classic case of a broken-down bureaucracy on one side and a clutch of aggrieved citizens on the other, plus a mayor with his precarious dignity. Sectarian animosities and suspicions would raise the stakes and the volume.

The manager of the Ministry began throwing down a long series of bureaucratic tripwires, booby traps, and obstacles. He had no authority to issue the food, he said. Authority would have to come from higher up, and who knew how long something like that might take, he said. There were protocols that couldn't be ignored, he said. And then there were the protocols that did not yet exist. And between the ones that could not be ignored and the ones that could not yet be followed there was no way to authorize the release of the food.

Earlier that morning, the Mayor had repeated the stories of other Baqubah officials who went on similar missions to Baghdad and never returned. He was sure that if the Americans were not present, he would already have been murdered. The man was in a cold sweat and his voice shook when he spoke.

The Shiite bureaucrats were dug in. They argued solo. They

argued in tag teams. More joined the fray. Soon the flying hands and soaring invectives were reminding me of Rome. It went on and on, reason after reason that Baqubah could have no food. At one point, Johnson interjected that there were children in Baqubah who needed to be fed. Apparently the protocol covering children hadn't been written yet. It began to look like we were not going to get any food today. Tomorrow was Friday; the warehouse would be closed.

The bureaucrats were unreasonable and unhelpful and were as much a part of Iraq's problems as was al Qaeda. But what we did not know at the time was that warehouses and silos in and around Baqubah were in fact loaded with grain, flour, and un-counted tons of sugar that al Qaeda had stolen. Even though the bureaucrats could not have known this for certain, they knew that al Qaeda had practically owned Baqubah, and was murder-ing Shiites by the thousands around Iraq. Why ship food out to Diyala province into the hands of the enemy? Arrowhead Ripper might have ripped out the heart of al Qaeda in Baqubah, but the spleen remained.

Finally a bureaucrat said it flatly: we would have to come back on Sunday. And then, suddenly, the Mayor spoke up. Faltering at first, the longer he talked, the more courage he mustered; the more courage he displayed, the more persuasive he became. John-son waited. When the Mayor seemed done, he said Prime Minis-ter Maliki and General Petraeus were watching to see what the Ministry of Trade would do. Johnson said he would not leave Baghdad without that food.

Johnson's ultimate threat was not the soldiers he had brought to Sadr City. His threat was shame. Johnson pointed to me, saying that he brought the press along so that the world would see the Ministry bureaucrats for what they were: either heroes or villains. Maybe other reporters would have been offended, or felt used, but Johnson was simply telling the truth. I *was* taping the meeting.

Whether it was Johnson's implied threat about not leaving without the food, or the vanity of the Iraqi bureaucrats when reminded they were being filmed for posterity, I'll never know. But it worked.

There were still hours of paperwork to do. The bureaucrats asked Johnson if he wanted to come back, but everyone sensed that would be unwise. So we waited. The soldiers kept guard. Hours passed. We were on the edge of Sadr City where we could be attacked at any moment. As the paperwork crept along, we ended up sitting with the bureaucrats and listening to their war stories about when they had been in the Iraqi Army. One man showed us scars from a mortar; another had spent years as an Iranian prisoner.

While we talked, one of our Strykers outside was attacked with a grenade. Apparently someone tried to throw it in the hatch (sometimes they get lucky), but missed. The grenade was loud, but everyone was OK. The paperwork had just been completed, so this was a good time to leave.

We returned to Baqubah with dozens of trucks of food. When the convoy finally arrived in Baqubah, the local media were waiting. Johnson gave full credit to the other leaders. It was straight out of a Bruce Willis movie: Johnson saved the day, then slipped quietly from the spotlight to make sure the Mayor and the Governor got all the credit. Nobody mentioned Tonto.

After the food came the fuel, water, and electricity, and each project was its own tangled mess. Johnson could often be heard saying things like, "Where is Tonto? *Call him!*" Tonto, who looked like he might weigh one hundred and twenty-five pounds, if he had just eaten and his pockets were full of sand, always managed to rally the courage and confidence of his fellow Iraqis. Over time more Tontos emerged.

After the adventure with the trucks, I'd see the Mayor out walking on the streets, people eager to talk with him. He was a bona fide media hero. And a much better mayor, according to Johnson, who later wrote to tell me how well the man had done:

"It was my experience that many mayors are selected to be lackeys and push the status quo—Abdullah wasn't that way. He wanted the best for Baqubah. He also had an extraordinary number of contacts in the city (probably from driving the bus)—seemed he knew everybody. He always had a full house for Muhtar meetings and we made a lot of progress when he chaired them. . . . He continued to demonstrate courage, especially as we experienced more and more success in his area of responsibility, which was the reconstruction and administration of Baqubah. I liked working with Abdullah, because I believed he had a good and honest heart and he was getting things done."

★ ★ ★

Early in 2008, I e-mailed LTC Johnson to ask about the longer-term impact of the convoy I'd accompanied to Baghdad in late June. His reply demonstrates another key to Johnson's success with counterinsurgency, because he continually monitored all the operations to ensure that things he had set in motion were still moving:

> After the first food shipments came in, we learned that simply getting the food to the people was not sufficient. The PDS was as much a symbol of the government's ability to function and serve the people as it was about providing sustenance. As a result, we focused our efforts on 're-teaching' (while learning ourselves) how the PDS (Public Distribution System) worked, so the government could provide the food in the manner it did prior to the invasion—all in an attempt to establish normalcy. Food shipments from Baghdad became more frequent, and we all worked hard getting food agents, using Iraqi Security to

distribute the food. We also had to empty the warehouse in Baqubah of 2006 food so it could accommodate the newer shipments.

A key aspect of this process was identified—Baqubah had the ability to mill and process rice and flour, the key components of the PDS. So the last thirty days of our time there was devoted to getting the mills running. This required more work with GoI and the State Department to get wheat to Baqubah, but with the help of GEN Petraeus and MG Rollo, we started getting the wheat. On the day we left, our team ate bread made from flour produced at a mill that had been abandoned for over a year (the wheat was from the U.S. by the way). Getting the mills up and running was as significant as anything we did in the area of essential services, because it demonstrated that the Diyala government could take care of itself.

I recalled something one of the Baghdad bureaucrats had said. Upon hearing that al Qaeda had scattered like rats out of Baqubah, he seemed at first not to believe that news, but once he got confirmation he made a point to say, "If al Qaeda was done in Baqubah, al Qaeda was done in Iraq." That wasn't entirely correct, but it was close.

CHAPTER THIRTEEN

How Hills Get Taken

Following the thrashing al Qaeda received in Baqubah during Operation Arrowhead Ripper, the survivors found themselves on the run and playing defense. They were reacting, while American and Iraqi forces pursued them not pell-mell, but methodically, deliberately, trying to shape the enemy into ever-small habitats. Al Qaeda increasingly moved up into the Diyala River valley, for instance. But history had shown how little time al Qaeda needed to regroup, re-supply, and set up new bases of operation. General Petraeus was determined not to give them any slack. "Stay after them," I heard Petraeus tell his commanders. "We've got our teeth in them," he once told me. It was true. Even in and around Baqubah, the fighting was far from done. Too often in the war the terrorists had been driven out of certain areas only until our forces moved on. Then the terrorists came back and began sawing off the heads of people who had cooperated. We had taught the people and al Qaeda that the U.S. was just passing through but al Qaeda is forever. The terrorists clearly hoped for a repeat in Baqubah with al Qaeda moving just beyond our immediate area of control and keeping at it.

The alliance with 1920s Revolution Brigades would get a severe test during July 2007, as American and Iraqi soldiers worked to root al Qaeda out of areas influenced by the 1920s. Alliances with former insurgents had worked brilliantly in Anbar, but I was cautious about whether we could duplicate that in Diyala. The 1920 Revolution Brigades were a particularly proficient enemy who remained committed to seeing American forces withdrawn from Iraq as soon as possible. Had al Qaeda demonstrated any sense of decency, the 1920s fighters might still be allied with them and against us. In fact, if al Qaeda had any moral compass whatsoever and discipline among their ranks, they might have beaten us in Iraq after our 2004 travesties.

I stayed with soldiers from Alpha Company 1-12 CAV in downtown Baqubah at a place called Combat Outpost White Castle. They were preparing for combat the next day (July 15), clearing a still-dangerous palm grove along the Diyala River, where seven suspected enemy had just been killed by American special operations forces. Among the dead were said to be several members of Tonto the truck driver's family.

American soldiers needed to link up with 1920s to swap information for future missions, so we rolled into downtown Baqubah. Daylight streamed through periscopes into the otherwise dark, hot Bradley packed with soldiers ready to burst out onto the open Baqubah road as soon as the ramps dropped. Once out, the soldiers sprinted for cover. Although the heat was extreme, it was better than in the back of the Bradley where there was no air-conditioning noise, darkness, and the prospect of being trapped in tangled wreckage, burning alive. But now we were out, and finding scant cover on the garbage- and metal-strewn streets in a place Mad Max might have felt at home. The place looked like sniperville. It was like deer hunting where the bucks have the rifles.

The soldiers spread out, and began moving. Every building was scarred by war. The streets were mostly vacant and filled with garbage. Every part of every building, every abandoned tire or crushed can could be a bomb. Everywhere are sharp, jagged traps. Every cut risked infection from drug-resistant bugs. Snipers could shoot from afar and melt away.

Block after block we moved. The soldiers had brought along an officer who was not infantry and who was not ready for the heat and combat movement. He was having serious trouble and looked as though he might collapse, so they slowed down. Soon we met up with the 1920s. I counted nineteen men, outfitted with AK-47s and ammo pouches. Our guys did not trust the 1920s, but admitted they were good at killing al Qaeda. And the 1920s were working to reconstruct Baqubah. They were involved with water projects and other civic affairs, at least to some extent. They had goals beyond killing; they weren't just a gang.

A few months earlier we had called them terrorists, but on that day, we called them Concerned Local Nationals (CLNs, or CLCs [Concerned Local Citizens], or neighborhood watches, militias, or today in 2008, "Sons of Iraq" [SOI]). Before I left Baqubah they would formalize a neighborhood watch group called "The Baqubah Guardians." (Little wonder why so many people at home have a hard time keeping track.) They did not have uniforms. Many wished to join the police but had not been hired yet, and the Shia-led government was erecting obstacles to hiring Sunni.

The enemy was good at copying Iraqi and Coalition uniforms. So we used simple recognition symbols, good only for one day. The far recognition signal for that day was a red piece of tape bound around the arm. One of the 1920s guys smiled as he tied a piece of red tape around my arm. For close recognition, for instance, a car might have a tiny piece of red tape. With all the 1920s guys wearing at least a tiny sliver of red on their clothing—running shoes with a tiny red stripe, a cap with red writing, or a shirt with a red logo—it looked like a St. Valentine's Day parade.

Anthony H. Cordesman, a professor whose expertise in Middle East and South Asia security matters is highly regarded in academic, government and defense circles, wrote about the 1920s in a report entitled *Iraq's Sunni Insurgents: Looking Beyond al Qaeda.*

"[The] 1920 Revolution Brigades was established in June 2003. The group is comprised of former Iraqi Army officers, and is an umbrella organization for over a dozen 'brigades.' The group denies connection to the Ba'ath Party. [. . .] Its primary objective was to drive Coalition forces from Iraq and establish a nationalist government with Islamic values, including justice and equality."

Standing in that courtyard with at least nineteen men of the 1920s, I wondered if there was any truth to that. Looking over to where they sat on the grass, I saw a book and asked one of the 1920s guys about it. Through an interpreter, he told me it was a book of Islamic verses that gave instructions on how to live a proper—as in righteous—life. I remembered how Abu Ali had explained the break with al Qaeda in terms of their sham version of Islam. The 1920s had been founded by Harith Dhahir Khamis al-Dari, the nephew and namesake of Harith al-Dari, the exiled head of the Muslim Scholars Association.

Cordesman's paper went on to describe the 1920s:

"The ideology of the group was to implement the law of Allah on earth and to rid Muslims of any deviations and non-Islamic practices. It has sworn to continue jihad until they have achieved victory or martyrdom."

The report stated: "It cooperates against U.S. and Iraqi forces and those who worked for them. It does not attack civilians or vital infrastructure and does not permit attacks on schools. The group claimed it has carried out over 5,000 attacks in 2006, killing over 2,000 U.S. troops, and wounding more than 7,000. It operates in Anbar, Baghdad, and Diyala."

Unlike al Qaeda, the 1920s had self-imposed boundaries on their behavior. They wanted to kick us out of Iraq and shape their own futures with their own hands. When al Qaeda announced that it had changed its name to the Islamic State of Iraq and moved its caliphate from Ramadi to Baqubah, it asked all the Sunni insurgent groups and militias to officially sign on and pledge allegiance. Because the 1920s were large, well organized, and effective, al Qaeda wanted the signature of Harith al-Dari, the 1920s founder, at the top of the list. He refused and was assassinated in an ambush near Abu Ghraib on March 27, 2007. By the end of that month, thirty other 1920s leaders met a similar end. By April, most of the 1920s branches in Iraq had made formal alliances with Coalition forces.

And so there we were, working alongside members of a proven, wily, and worthy adversary making plans to kill some al Qaeda together. After our meeting we returned to COP White Castle. No showers, crowded conditions. The soldiers began to prepare for our mission the next day by clearing that dangerous palm grove. We would be working not with the 1920s but some Iraqi Army. Watching our soldiers carefully check and recheck each other's gear made me feel more comfortable about going with them on a dangerous mission.

One soldier asked who would carry the Holy Hand Grenade, and everyone laughed. Fragmentation grenades, or "frags," are dangerous to carry and use. Soldiers wrap tape around the pin top and tape on the lever despite being told not to. Young soldiers are allowed to carry them only in the most dangerous environments. It's very easy to accidentally kill yourself or a buddy with a frag.

Each of these soldiers carried two frags, so I knew we were expecting serious combat.

After all the preparations, a few soldiers worked out, using MRE cases for a bench. As it approached 9:00 P.M., the briefings for platoon and squads wrapped up. Hydrate and hydrate some more. The next day would bring a hot and dangerous mission. And there would be death. There were so many ways to get killed.

How to Get Killed

I heard my danger chimes when we dropped ramp in the "Mechanix" section of Baqubah and linked up with some Iraqi soldiers. Minutes after we hit the ground—POW!—a shot fired close by kicked dust into the air. An Iraqi soldier had accidentally fired his AK-47. I already had suspicions that these particular Iraqi soldiers weren't squared-away, which that shot confirmed. But it wasn't like 2005 when I would seek cover whenever Iraqi Army approached. They were getting better and some units had become excellent fighting forces.

We headed out to the palm groves. It was dangerously hot in all the gear. And now down along the river was the humidity. Mosquitoes must sweat here.

We walked and walked, and a soldier kept asking me if I was OK. I kept saying I would be carrying him before he would be carrying me. One of the tricks to combat reporting is you don't have to be tougher than all the soldiers, just tougher than one. When the first one collapses, and they stop to stick an IV into him, you also get a break.

The following day, three soldiers would collapse from the heat during some fighting, and two of them were so dehydrated that their veins collapsed, proving once again that you don't have to be tougher than everyone, just the guys who don't drink enough water. I drank water like a fish and dived for every sliver of shade, thinking of the body like a battery that gets drained quickly by the heat and sun.

Al Qaeda still lurked in the area, so the farmers were happy to see us. One woman said that seeing the army out there was a blessing from God, which made the soldiers happy.

Much food was growing—juicy grapes and dates. I was getting hungry, but I felt a twinge of danger. Couldn't quite put my finger on it; just a feeling that something unexpected might happen.

This was a perfect place for al Qaeda, where a savage enemy could live, terrorizing the people, making slaves of them, with a steady supply of food nearby and ready access to bomb-making materials.

During the mission, we kept hearing shots maybe a quarter-mile away, and there were also some large bombs exploding in the further distance. Voices over the radio said some were just IEDs being destroyed by our forces.

Eventually we worked our way through a village, then down the Diyala River, which flows toward Baghdad. The Diyala is an old river without much slope in this area, and so it twists and bows several times in and through Baqubah. All along the river, as on all Iraqi waterways, people suck out the water, taking far more than they need, and complain about the people upriver who do the same.

We took a break beside the river. Soldiers from the 5th Iraqi Army started spray-painting the outside wall of an Iraqi house to show they had been there. Captain Sheldon Morris heard the hiss of the spray paint and told them to stop painting people's property.

Iraqi soldiers were nearly always embarrassed when an American like CPT Morris told them to cut out the idiocy. But they weren't just embarrassed; discipline earned their respect. Before the war, our people had no street credibility in Iraq. Iraqis thought American soldiers were soft and that body armor was a type of personal air conditioner. If the Iraqis had known back then what they knew by this time about American willingness to suffer and fight, it's doubtful that Saddam would have taunted us.

Of course we swept them off the main battlefields quickly, but that could be and often was chalked up to our money and our machines. It was only after, when they saw that our people were better street fighters, too, and that American combat soldiers would match or outlast them in the heat, that they began to understand. At this point, the man-to-man respect was there. And so, when someone like CPT Morris told Iraqi soldiers to stop doing idiotic things to people's property, something they already knew was wrong, their respect for Americans grew. Day after day, Iraqis came to Americans asking for justice, because they saw men like CPT Sheldon Morris act justly and make their justice stick with strength. In Iraq our military has come to be viewed as a great tribe.

The break was over. We'd been out for some hours. We kept hearing fighting, which seemed to be slightly downriver. CPT Morris, monitoring communications, told us that the Bradleys that had dropped us off had been watching some activity down in the direction of the gunfire. We continued the clearing, but the sound of gunfire continued.

At 9:59 P.M., a Bradley reported a silver van carrying several men who had dropped off a large white sack on Route Burga, perhaps a few hundred meters to our south, and then drove off heading west. Route Burga had not been cleared yet and could have been riddled with IEDs, but we were heading there. We weren't aware at the time that some 1920s guys had been in a firefight with al Qaeda in the area with at least one 1920s guy reported killed.

At around 10:05 P.M. we started moving to contact (meaning:

trying to engage in the fight). We walked south, moving toward the firing, linking up with SGT Michael's squad and the IA with him. By now the fighting was a few hundred meters away. All small arms. I didn't hear any explosions. Some civilians had been caught in the crossfire and a woman was shot in the neck and slightly wounded, though we did not yet know this. The fighting was light: maybe one machine gun and four or five AK-47s. But often small actions turn into big fights as other elements, friendly and enemy, are drawn in.

We approached a wide-open field and could see Route Burga perhaps a couple of hundred yards in front of us. Staff Sergeant Le gave the hand signal for everyone to cross the open area in an inverted wedge formation. We were accompanied by dozens of Iraqi soldiers. They recognized the signal and also got into the wedge.

As we crossed the field, at about 10:20 P.M., the silver van started driving in front of us. We could see it driving from our right to our left on Route Burga a couple of hundred meters away. The van was well within small-arms range. I was unaware of the radio chatter about the armed men in the van, or the white sack they had dropped; so to me it was just a van that was driving near us with four men, while a firefight was going on nearby. But to Captain Morris and the others hearing the radio chatter, and to those soldiers in the Bradleys peering with excellent optics, the men in the van were clearly armed and not displaying any sort of recognition signal. The van was in an area where there was fighting going on, and where American special operations forces had killed enemy in the past twenty-four hours, and where we knew that al Qaeda was lurking.

One of the Bradleys saw what he thought were bullets kicking up in our direction, as if someone were shooting at us. But at that time—the silver van now nearly directly in front of us—I heard no shots and saw no contact. As the van closed the range at about two hundred meters, our guys fired several warning shots. The van sped up. The soldiers rained heavy small-arms fire and were kicking up dust, and Corporal Anthony Johnson fired a 40mm grenade, but the van just kept speeding away. Slugs kicked up dust, some bullets struck the van, but it kept going. The van was getting away. A Bradley gunner had been tracking the van in his crosshairs but holding fire. He squeezed the trigger on his 25mm cannon.

BAMBAMBAMBAM!!!!

Concussion from the 25mm shots slapped the ground and popped up moon dust around the Bradley. Like a giant jackhammer. Each bullet weighs about four times more than a golf ball, and traveling thousands of feet per second, 25mm shots are devastating to human bodies. A single shot can pop a man into barely recognizable chunks and bits. The four bullets traveled at nearly one mile per second toward the van in front of us. Each bullet contained explosives. The first 25mm penetrated above the right rear tail light leaving a bowling-ball-sized hole, exploding inside with a brief fireball. A benefit of explosive rounds is that after they explode they don't travel a mile or two and possibly whack someone who was not involved.

All four rounds hit the van and exploded, and the vehicle careened off the road and crashed out of sight.

A woman rushed out to the van and scarfed up an AK and ran away into a nearby palm grove. Staff Sergeant Le had her in his sights, but did not fire, though she was now considered an armed combatant. Le could have killed her, but I don't remember ever seeing a soldier intentionally take a shot at a woman, even when it would have been legal to do so, as now.

As we moved out toward the van, there were reports that some of the guys had gone into a house. At first our guys were going to attack the house, but that report apparently was wrong. At the same time, the woman who had been shot in the neck by someone else came running to us, screaming for help. She could have been wearing a suicide vest; women sometimes do. But apparently nobody sensed danger from her, nor did I. The medic went to work on her. Fortunately it was only a flesh wound, but I always find it amazing that so many Iraqi civilians will run to American soldiers even during firefights. She was tough and just wanted to sit down with Americans where it was safe. Sort of safe. A few soldiers stayed back with her and for security to watch the area, while the rest of us kept closing in on the area where the van crashed. We were now on Route Burga, which had not been cleared. Our guys could all be blown to pieces, but they kept moving forward. The van might have been meant to lure us onto the road, and we all knew it, and we were now on the road.

Al Qaeda operatives often wear suicide vests, and given the way al Qaeda fights, our guys would have been justified in calling the Bradley forward and ordering it to obliterate the van. Clearly the guys were armed and those who were still alive were also still combatants. Instead, at great risk to their own lives, our guys moved forward toward the van without just destroying it.

They kept closing in. This was fantastically dangerous. I remember wondering what their families might think about them moving in to take the guys alive, when this could cost their own lives. How would I write about these soldiers if they were blown up by a suicide vest or gigantic bomb (a big bomb would get me too) planted specifically to take advantage of their sense of decency? This is why counterinsurgency is hard and dangerous, but also why it works. By walking to the van, by not taking life unnecessarily, by risking their own lives to avoid killing, our guys were taking the moral high ground. Taking the moral high ground, like taking a hill, often means exposing yourself to death in ways that might seem foolish. I won't say "heroic" because soldiers hate that word. But that's how hills get taken.

All four of the Iraqi men were kitted out (wearing ammo pouches and so forth), and two AKs were found. One AK was on the scene, and the woman had run off with the other, the woman Staff Sergeant Le didn't shoot. Instead, another group of soldiers entered her home, got the AK and left her and the family alone.

Before the medics could go to work, the four guys who had been hit had to be searched. Hand grenades could be in any pocket.

The driver was one hundred percent dead. His body was blasted partially outside the van, his foot caught by the steering wheel leaving him hanging upside down, oozing and dripping blood and bodily fluids into the parched earth.

An army medic treated the wounded. One man was moaning and groaning. He was badly wounded, having been hit in the testicles, among other injuries. Another man had a sucking chest wound, with air going through a hole directly into the lungs. His lung was filling with blood and he was drowning. Two medics tried to plug the hole in his back. But it was too late. The man died.

Iraqi men approached waving a white flag, which often has been used as a ploy to attack our people. One of them had a bandage on his left hand. (I would recognize him in the next day's fighting by that hand.) They wanted to tell us that the men we shot were their friends in the 1920s. The men who approached us were detained at gunpoint, treated well but flex-cuffed on the ground, given ice-cold water. But they were telling the truth. They were 1920s fighters as we later learned. The Iraqi men had been gutsy to approach us like that, and to see what we did to their friends and to vouch for them. American soldiers brought the flex-cuffed men back to COP White Castle. An American soldier noticed that one man was in pain, so the soldier cut the flex-cuffs and told the him to keep his hands behind his back. After some hours, they were all released.

In an honest case of mistaken identity and miscommunication, we had killed two men from a very skilled, deadly, and not especially pro-American insurgent group with which we had an uneasy alliance. We were supposed to join up with the same group the next morning to hunt for al Qaeda.

CHAPTER FOURTEEN

Seven Rules and An Oath

Next morning our soldiers assembled by the Bradleys for the pre-mission briefing. The mission would link up with Iraqi Army and 1920s fighters we'd accidentally pummeled. Some Americans did not want to go on the mission. They didn't trust the 1920s guys, and the sky was too hazy for medevac helicopters.

We headed back down into the danger zone after much hot and dangerous movement to the link-up spot. The 1920s guys were late, again, and wanted us to come to them, but the lieutenants in charge of our patrol said no, let the 1920s come to us. We stayed at an intersection for what seemed like an hour, but probably was only thirty minutes. I scanned the area for danger and found it in every angle. Small IEDs are easy to emplace. Hidden bombs can be set in just a minute. If the enemy can predict which way we are going, and get in front of us, they can kill us. That means threats are everywhere. A car tire could pack enough explosives to obliterate us. One of the many shops along the way could be stacked to the ceiling with explosives. Powerful bombs could be hidden in bike frames and then the bike could be quickly leaned on a wall in front of us. Hand grenades could be thrown over walls. Some walls could be packed with explosives on the other side.

Urban combat is among the most stressful environments in the world. Small holes can be punched through walls where an AK barrel can suddenly stick through. The enemy can make dozens of holes in the walls, keeping camouflaged, and then suddenly dozens of AKs are firing.

We could hear a family in a nearby home wailing for the men killed yesterday. They treated us well, but our own soldiers were callous about it. Maybe they had seen too much death, but their reaction seemed cold to me.

The 1920s guys sent a kid on a bicycle with a message that we should go to them, but again the two lieutenants wisely refused, and finally said to hell with it. We would do the mission with the Iraqi Army alone. We began walking.

We were in a high sniper-threat area. If rockets or mortars came down, luck and God were our only shields.

We walked beside the river. If fire comes and you dive for cover and fall into water too deep, the heavy gear you carry can drown you.

As we began moving toward our objective, we passed house after house. Empty, well-kept houses are always a bad sign. Well-kept means there are people living there. Empty means those people may know something we would like to know. The homes were well kept. Many were empty. And al Qaeda was almost certainly out there trying to predict which way we would walk. I knew it. Could feel it.

When we had to check out a house, instead of breaking the gates open, an Iraqi soldier would crawl over the walls and open the gates. Very dangerous because the soldier would make a great target going over the wall. The Iraqi soldiers did not ransack any of the houses and were respectful of the property. They were improving in more ways than just combat.

It's important to stay away from the soldiers carrying rockets. During combat, a soldier might whip the RPG around quickly and fire, and if you are on the backside of the launcher, the blast and burns can be lethal. There was an RPG-toting Iraqi who seemed to like to be close to the camera, so I had to keep my eye on him lest he accidentally kill me.

We were told there might be snipers waiting. The raised road we walked along was dangerous, so one of our two platoons headed out to cover the left flank.

The day grew hotter and hotter until it felt like my eyes were sweating and hours melted and dripped away. While we moved down the road—*POW!*—a shot was fired that seemed to come from the palm groves to our left. But that was where the other American platoon was covering our left flank.

Then an American soldier opened fire into the palm grove— in the direction of our other platoon. Other members of the platoon I was with descended upon him like hawks. But the American soldier just laughed until he got tackled by another soldier, as Iraqi soldiers stood watching with mouths agape. Finally, the lieutenant sent the errant soldier back to the Bradleys. Before tensions could escalate, the 1920s guys arrived.

The American soldiers weren't comfortable with the 1920s guys around, but I could see that the 1920s were not just a bunch of yahoos. The way they carried themselves and moved together telegraphed that many had been soldiers. They had control of the muzzles of their weapons, and their fingers were not on the triggers. Their weapons were all clean. I noticed one of the 1920s had a very clean ammunition belt. Untrained soldiers usually will not clean the machine gun ammunition, but his was sparkling. They kept intervals like good soldiers.

One of the 1920s recognized me. He was the one who had been detained the day before when the two men got shot to death, and he was the one whose hand had been hurt. He came up and showed me his hand: his thumb had stitches and his face showed that he was still in pain. I pointed him toward the medic.

Some of the 1920s guys were about three hundred meters down the road when they walked into an ambush that had apparently been set for us. *BOOOOOMMMM!* I dove for cover as heavy small-arms fire began, and I could also hear machine guns. The bomb was big, and I was sure it must have killed five or ten of them. But soon they started streaming back, dazed and agitated, some with clothes tattered from the blast. None had been killed. They were alive because they were good and serious soldiers. Had they been walking in a group instead of keeping their intervals, that explosion had been big enough to scatter their body parts all over the road and up into the trees. The man whose clean ammunition belt had caught my eye earlier was now dragging it down the road. I walked up and pointed to it and he nodded and draped the belt back on his shoulder where it should be. The shooting continued. Thousands of bullets were snapping around. Part of my video of that day ran on *Good Morning America*. Most Americans were probably having a better morning.

As we broke contact the heat was tearing into people. Three American soldiers crumpled—two of them seriously—their veins had collapsed. Iraqi soldiers and the 1920s were staggering from the heat. They live here and none of them were carrying as much weight as our guys. Other 1920s and IA dove for shade and stopped moving.

We rushed to get the three heat casualties back to FOB Warhorse. Serious heat casualties are just as life-threatening as bullet wounds. Medics and doctors were waiting and got right to work. That day, at least, no American blood was shed, which was miraculous given all the flying bullets. I got out of the Bradley heat and into the sunlight's heat and started back to my tent. One of the soldiers said, "Hey, where you goin'?" as if I was abandoning them. "Walking back," I said. "Get in the Bradley and we'll take you there."

I thought, "Don't get me started on how unbearable it is inside the Bradley, these guys think the Bradley is the best thing since the flying saucer." The Strykers are air-conditioned; they include legroom and are deadlier for infantry fighting. Don't even bother telling this to a Bradley soldier. It's hopeless and they might never invite you out again. Just before we dropped ramp again, I asked the soldier sitting in front of me, "Why did that guy shoot into the palm grove?"

Anger flashed over his face as he stared at the soldier sitting to my left.

"He's sitting right beside you, why don't you ask him?"

I hadn't realized he was sitting next to me.

"Why did you shoot?" I asked accusingly. I was as upset as the soldiers were, but this soldier was treating it like a joke, laughing about it, talking about how he could get sent home. He was the only one laughing. I wanted him to go to jail and laugh about it there.

When the ramp dropped, soldiers from other Bradleys piled out and started yelling at him. They were still yelling at him as I started walking away in the scorching dust.

After two days and two missions where mistakes were made, where some men died, and others dropped from a heat so intense that it blurred the already fine line between friends and enemies, where new alliances between old enemies were tested under fire, these soldiers were not so tired or so worn from the heat as to let their standards flag: they were all over the one soldier who did.

Later I would learn that the suspicions about Tonto's family were wrong. They'd been among those seven Iraqis shot by American Special Operations soldiers in a firefight along the Diyala River, but they were not al Qaeda members or sympathizers. Tonto, as LTC Fred Johnson would tell me, was an Iraqi police officer. He was also a Shiite, as were all the members of his family in Baqubah. Prior to the launch of Operation Arrowhead Ripper, the Iraqi police in Baqubah had not been paid in almost a year. While on vacation, Tonto started up his trucking business.

For all the persistent suspicion among our soldiers about the 1920s fighters, so far they'd demonstrated an impressive commitment to the alliance. We'd destroyed their van, killed two of their guys, wounded two others, and detained a group who were trying to help identify the men we'd just shot. Today, their guys had shown up after burying friends, put up with a cold reception from our guys on a hot day, and by taking a lead position in our march, took a bomb meant for us.

Seven Rules and An Oath

Despite the lack of warmth between soldiers and 1920s, the work in Baqubah was a clear success on many fronts, from combat operations to reconstruction projects, from mentoring local leaders to formal institutional reform that happened from the ground up. In Baqubah, all these dots connected up with Seven Rules and One Oath.

Colonel Steve Townsend, the American commander of the 3-2 Stryker Brigade Combat Team, presided over a meeting with Iraqi Army officers and former insurgent leaders, now collectively referred to as the "Baqubah Guardians."

COL Townsend's staff had prepared a slideshow that started off with a draft of Seven Rules. The final version of the Seven Rules was open to discussion and suggestions from those in attendance. The rules were to be followed by an oath, also still in draft form.

After the proposal for the Seven Rules and An Oath were presented, the most interesting—fascinating, really—part of the meeting unfolded. The Iraqi Army commanders and Baqubah Guardians took it all very seriously. First, they gave input on all seven proposed rules:

1) Protect your community from AQI, JAM, and other terrorist militia.

Some attendees did not like that AQI and JAM were singled out, arguing this actually showcased those organizations, while slighting the problems from other terrorist groups. Other attendees disagreed and thought the groups should be named, but finally it was decided to strike the names AQI and JAM.

2) Accept peaceful Sunni, Shia, and others.

After some intelligent discussion, the Iraqis wanted this changed to "Accept all peaceful Iraqi citizens without discrimination."

3) Stay in your neighborhood/AO (area of operations) for your safety.

This needed clarification. Colonel Townsend was not saying people should not travel from their neighborhoods, but that they should not operate out of their neighborhoods, to which the attendees agreed.

4) Take an oath of allegiance to the Constitution of Iraq.

Then it got interesting. One Iraqi said that even under the Saddam regime, bad as it was, the constitution still kept them together. He went on to say that the current constitution tended to divide Iraq. As more Iraqis joined in, arguing the merits or flaws with the constitution, it was clear this rule could lead to months or years of debate. Townsend tabled it for now.

5) Register with Iraqi security forces and Coalition forces (biometrics for CF).

The biometrics was an issue partly because Coalition forces do not share biometrics with the Iraqi Security Forces. Therefore we were asking Iraqis to submit to photographing, fingerprinting, and retinal scanning for our use only. The Iraqis politely offered that this was not a good idea. Colonel Townsend chuckled, saying even Americans wouldn't go for that.

6) For your safety, wear a standard uniform and markings (an example was proposed).

The uniform idea was fine with the Iraqis, especially since we had killed at least six of their militia members in the last thirty days.

7) Receive hiring preferences for Iraqi Police and Army.

This rule was unanimously approved. Although I'd been harsh in my judgment of the Iraqi Police, I later learned from LTC Fred Johnson that there were mitigating factors:

> The problem with the police was that they were poorly equipped and trained; they weren't being paid and there weren't enough of them for a city the size of Baqubah. This was . . . being worked out when we left. The Guardians were being hired on slowly to fill the shortage of IPs, but there was a lot of bureaucracy that was weighing down the process.

On the oath, the discussion was even more interesting, especially after experiencing the tension between factions on those back-to-back missions.

1) I will support and defend the Constitution of Iraq.

2) I will cooperate fully with the Iraqi government.

This point received some pushback because the central government in Baghdad had not proved dependable, fair, or even competent as far as the people in Baqubah could tell.

The other points were subject to brief discussions and easier agreement, although the easiest was point six: "I will not support sectarian agendas." Every Iraqi in the room was onboard for this one and seemed enthusiastic about it. No one fought to keep their own separate allegiances, because everyone had already experienced the chaos that results.

During the presentation, the Iraqi flag appeared on some of the slides, but without the traditional words "Allahu Akbar," or "God is Great." This was a potentially serious faux pas. It was said that Saddam had put God is Great on the flags so that Iraqis would stop grinding the flags into the dirt with their feet; he knew Iraqis would never trample on those words. But there were no outbursts. Everyone was calm, professional, and very polite. An Iraqi colonel generously offered that he believed it to be just a mistake that God is Great was left off the flag on the slides being shown. But the Iraqis all agreed that no one was going to sign anything that displayed an Iraqi flag without that phrase.

This might seem ominous to Americans who, watching the news, hear angry men shouting, "Allahu Akbar!" while threatening America with endless fire. But to the Iraqis the issue was more like the strong feelings Americans have over the issue of printing "In God We Trust" on American currency. Months later, I asked Fred Johnson if they ever finished the oath and rules and whether it had held up as a way to build consensus and knit together the civil and social fabric. Johnson told me that all CLN (Concerned Local Nationals; aka CLC; Baqubah Guardians; Sons of Iraq, et al.) leaders had taken the oath and had administered it to their men. It wasn't without some contention. But Johnson saw the contention as part of government leaders learning to balance competing interests while keeping people focused on common goals. As he explained:

"After the oath, the CLNs developed a chain of command with open association with several key leaders in the Diyala government. For the most part they abided by the terms of the oath, but there were some instances where the CLNs broke rules, such as wearing identification, etc., which resulted in some confusion during engagements—none resulted in death as far as I know. There was some in-fighting between some CLN leaders, but the key was getting the government leaders to broker the disagreements."

Operation Arrowhead Ripper had launched on June 19, 2007. In July we were cleaning the remnants of al Qaeda out from the area around Baqubah. That first food convoy, which really marked the beginning of the rebuilding of civil order in the city, had arrived shortly thereafter. By the end of the summer, Baqubah had made enormous strides back toward a normal existence. Al Qaeda was on the run almost everywhere, soon to retreat on Mosul as they had in the past. Much was left to be done, but the transformation that had been wrought in less than a year, starting with the Anbar Awakening in the fall of 2006, was on the order of a miracle.

In September 2007, I went back to the United States for a few weeks and found a nation not at all inclined to believe in miracles. I was struck by the bizarre contrast between what most Americans seemed to think was happening in Iraq versus what I had just seen. My countrymen seemed to be living under a glass dome that allowed few hard facts to filter in unless attached to a string of false assumptions or skewed to a convenient ideology. My trip coincided with General Petraeus's testimony before the U.S. Congress, when media interest in the war was (I'm told) much greater than it had been for months. Translation: Britney was competing for airtime with O. J. in one of the saddest sideshows on Earth.

I watched the Senate hearings on September 11. Senators, one assumes, are more focused on the war than on O. J., or even Britney. But the hearing made it clearer that there was a tremendous gulf between what was actually happening in Iraq and what people in America thought was happening. It was as if the inertia of bad news from the previous three years had made it impossible to take in new information.

As Petraeus patiently explained, across Iraq trends were positive. Attacks on Coalition forces had decreased significantly; sectarian violence was down. The Sunni Awakening movement had spread from Anbar to other provinces. Moqtada al Sadr had ordered his Shiite militias to cease fire, and those who were still fighting were being targeted by his Golden Groups. When Sheik Sattar was murdered in September 2007, days after Petraeus's testimony, it was a sad day for his people, but not a setback for the movement itself. It only made the Sunni of Anbar more resolved to fight al Qaeda.

The response to all this: General Petraeus was told that his testimony, like all good fiction, required "a willing suspension of disbelief."

One problem was that it wasn't really possible to explain why we were winning now without laying out in excruciating detail why we had been losing before. That wasn't the general's job, and the people whose job it was showed no inclination to do it. Maybe they still did not understand.

We'd spent billions of dollars to protect ourselves against roadside bombs in Iraq, while mostly failing to cultivate the most effective defense of all: an Iraqi citizen with a cell phone. We spent hundreds of billions of dollars on combat operations that might have been avoided if we'd learned from our successes in Mosul in 2003, rather than compounding the blunders of 2004.

But then we'd gotten, miraculously, our second chance. And we were making the most of it. Cell phones? Iraqis are e-mailing our guys Google Earth maps to show where the terrorists are. With the increasing support of citizens and the growing prowess of the Iraqi Army, American troops have been able not only to leverage their combat effectiveness but spend more time in cop-on-the-beat mode, building closer ties to their communities, which then translates into being more effective in working on local civil affairs issues.

Neighborhoods that had been war zones as late as July 2007 were now peaceful. Schools and markets had reopened. The scars of war were still visible everywhere—wrecked buildings, Jersey barriers and checkpoints, concertina wire, bullet holes and bomb craters. And there was still much work to be done. A few catastrophic attacks could have destroyed a great deal of progress, which is why in August, as a plan for this book was born, I told my publisher that it was far too early to declare victory. But it was definitely time to declare serious progress. It is said that we should learn from our mistakes. But success can teach us just as much. Many Americans, at least for the moment, seemed uninterested in that lesson.

I returned to Iraq convinced that if we didn't take our second chance and run with it as fast as we could, we—and our new friends in Iraq—would lose it forever.

General Petraeus seemed to have reached the same conclusion.

CHAPTER FIFTEEN

Men of Valor

Arm yourselves and be ye men of valor and be in readiness for the conflict, for it is better for us to perish in battle than to look upon the outrage of our nation and our altars.

WINSTON CHURCHILL

While America learned by bloody trial and error how to fight this war, our British allies had been operating in the overwhelmingly Shia south, facing very different challenges. At first that relatively peaceful region had been the easier task. Al Qaeda was not a factor in the south, nor was the south ever cracking under civil war as in places like Diyala province and Baghdad. Very broadly speaking, in the midsection of Iraq—from the ethnically mixed environs of Baghdad up roughly to the even-more ethnically mixed Mosul—many Iraqis first had welcomed us, or at least cooperated with us, then grew to resent and oppose us, with many resorting to an alliance with al Qaeda and other groups that expelled us.

Even at the worst of times, of course, we were not actively opposed by most Iraqis, or we would have lost the war very quickly. And even at the worst of times, more volunteers lined up for the Iraqi Army and Iraqi Police than could be absorbed. We have never been blood-enemies of Iraqis, and we are not today. We have become so much a part of the landscape that, in a nation in which lobbing a missile can be a fair-play negotiating tactic, we may be attacked by groups like JAM, not because they hate us, but because they want something from us. By late 2007, I kept hearing Iraqis ask, always joking, I think, when the American soldiers were going to join their tribe? American commanders in tribal meetings are often treated like especially important sheiks.

Even during the outrages of the Fallujah-flattenings and prisoner rape-torture debacles, Iraqis never turned against us the way they would later turn against al Qaeda. We were never completely evil in their eyes. Dumb, overbearing, disrespectful, but not evil. Even during the worst of times, we would pay for people's houses we flattened, and often treat Iraqis—whose ailments had nothing to do with war—in American clinics.

The dynamic of the tribes and the rational insurgents coming to us for help against al Qaeda did not operate in the south. Just when U.S. forces were being embraced by the sheiks and former insurgent groups like the 1920s, the Shia in the south, who did not need to be defended from al Qaeda, were growing increasingly restive. British forces were increasingly felt to be an irritant, though I have seen firsthand that the Brits are just as good with the people, and often better, than we had been. To their credit no one understood all this better than the British themselves, who adopted a conscious policy of pulling back from contact with the populace and making themselves as inconspicuous as possible. As the situation improved for us, the situation for the British in the south truly started to go south, and then they began to pull out of Iraq and focus more on Afghanistan. Al Qaeda tried to seize credit for expelling the Brits, but there were probably more Swedish blondes in Basra than there were al Qaeda. And the blondes were a lot safer.

The somewhat unfair result was that our greatest ally began to get into very serious fighting and then draw down significantly just as it began to seem that the story of the war might have a happy ending. But it would be unfair to leave our greatest allies out of this book. They did their part and then some. No nation was ever more blessed in its allies than we are in the Brits.

Combat in Basra

The British soldiers had been out longer than thirteen hours and the heat was stifling. Ambient temperature was now 115° F outside the vehicles, and temperatures approached 70° C (around 150° F) inside. Soldiers poured water down their body armor. The driver was naked other than his body armor and helmet, while soldiers in the back literally pulled down their pants. This was more than an attempt at comfort; they were trying not to die. Thick clouds of thick dust baked the putrid Basra odors until they could gag a goat, although by then the soldiers inside the Bulldogs and Warriors could have offered serious competition in a stink contest. With their heavy body armor and helmets, and laden with ammunition, rashes erupted on their skin. Their goggles and ballistic glasses were filthy. The place was like a toilet used as an oven. The people on the septic streets were flushed with hostility.

Five days before, the British unit 4 Rifles, commanded by Lieutenant Colonel Patrick Sanders, had begun their deployment in the British base at Basra Palace. (American units are typically designated by numbers, while British units have names.) On May 21, 4 Rifles was conducting its first mission in on Basra's deadly streets. On point as always were the one hundred twenty soldiers of Royal Welsh 2nd Battalion, also known as the "Rorke's Drift Company," the name earned after a legendary stand against a Zulu army in Natal, South Africa, in 1879 that outnumbered the Welsh more than thirty to one, for which more Victoria Crosses were awarded than for any other battle in British history. They are also known as the "Welsh Warriors." Rorke's Drift Company always takes point on the 4 Rifles patrols and convoys, because 4 Rifles mostly uses the older, armored Bulldogs whose electronics are not as well suited for spotting IEDs and other threats. Rorke's Drift, however, uses Warriors (similar to the American Bradley), with more sophisticated gear.

After fighting all night—thirteen hot, exhausting hours of near-constant fighting against a rested enemy, with no KIAs—exhausted of sleep and food, drained from the heat, 4 Rifles was escorting a resupply convoy of about two-dozen vehicles straight through the center of Basra. The British were mostly in armored vehicles. Armor dominates open terrain, but the advantages of armor begin to evaporate in cities.

The Shia militia Jaysh al-Mahdi was waiting ahead: there were about one hundred of them lying in ambush. The convoy was just nearing the Martyr Sadr building when the enemy opened fire with small arms and RPGs (rocket propelled grenades). Corporal Jeremy "Jez" Brookes, a vehicle commander, was shot in the head and died on the spot. Others were wounded.

Some enemy concentrated fire on a fuel transport driven by a Pakistani contractor whose son worked on base in Basra. The Pakistani driver was hit. His body slumped and fell from the truck, which soon caught fire—orange flames and black smoke filled the sky. An armed crowd surged into the street, among them women dressed in black. The crowd dragged away the body of the Pakistani driver. British soldiers tried to get to him, but there was too much combat. The driver disappeared and was never seen again.

As the convoy attempted to cross a bridge, a low-rider carrying a Land Rover and Saxon broke down, blocking it. PTE Paul Brinkworth, a young soldier with Rorke's Drift, 6th Platoon, knew instinctively that the bridge would be key to the battle, so without orders he turned his Warrior toward it. With bullets coming from all directions, popping off his armor and hitting the small shields of thick glass, Brinkworth stayed up in the hatch radioing key information to his commander and firing his rifle.

Meanwhile, Corporal Daly jumped out of his Warrior and ran from vehicle to vehicle, searching for British casualties. Like Brinkworth, nobody had given Daly orders. He just did it. When Daly reached one vehicle, he found that the commander had been shot in the head and was severely injured. After relaying the information to his company commander, it occurred to Daly that the young driver, Rifleman Brett Campbell, might need leadership after the shock of seeing his commander shot in the head. Daly ran back, got into the Warrior, and commanded it himself. He directed the driver over uncleared and unsecured routes out of the ambush.

Despite soldiers like Brinkworth and Daly, the British convoy was still in danger of further attack. Three vehicles were stuck on the bridge: the Land Rover, the Saxon, and the truck that carried them. If those vehicles were abandoned, the Brits would lose the media battle that would take place after the guns cooled. Media wins and losses in this war translate back to the battlefield just as readily as sterling converts to dollars. There is a clear battlefield conversion from ink to blood, from blood to ink. Even the younger British soldiers realized this, and they wanted to get those three vehicles off the bridge.

People who look at mechanics and think they only turn wrenches and get greasy from the safety of bases do not know the mechanics of the British and American armies. The mechanics' jobs may be even more inglorious than infantry, and even when commanders recognize the courage and critical value mechanics bring to battle after battle, nobody ever seems to believe it. The poor mechanics seemed resigned to a life of obscurity, but this writer can vouch that without them, in risking the roads of Iraq we would clunk to a dangerous halt.

The infantry needed a mechanic, so they radioed to Basra Palace where Lance Corporal Burn and Corporal Miller answered the call. Burn and Miller, both recovery mechanics (REME), headed to the fight in a completely unarmored recovery vehicle called a Foden. Burn and Miller were escorted about three miles to the bridge where they found themselves in the middle of a ferocious three-dimensional gun battle. An estimated seventy-five enemy were coming at the British from about fifteen to twenty positions, including a police station, rooftops, windows, and alleys. RPGs were exploding off Warriors and Bulldogs, which were firing everything they had, quickly running out of 30mm ammunition.

Captain Moger had moved his platoon into a perilous position. Nearly two-dozen enemy positions engaged him and his platoon in close contact from 360°. Bullets struck Moger's Warrior but to no effect. Even when the Warrior was blasted with six RPGs, nobody was hurt. The RPGs that would have wiped out a Humvee were not killing his men, but the heat was. Moger's gunner collapsed into the vehicle; the men inside were vomiting. It's not a far step from that to death, so he worked a quick plan to expedite getting those who needed medical assistance back to the palace, while he and his remaining men kept fighting. Moger was not about to leave the REMEs uncovered. He stayed in the fight, hitting approximately ten enemy with his own weapon before running low on ammo.

The noise was tremendous; smoke and dust obscured the battlefield. With infantry soldiers fighting and watching, what Burn and Miller did next was incredible.

The REMEs assessed the damage and started working, with bullets and RPGs splitting the air around them. They bled the brakes, with bullets striking close, some literally hitting just near their heads or kicking by their feet. RPGs struck the Land Rover and Saxon just meters away, while the men unhooked the trailer carrying them and cut the chains. Those watching thought it was a miracle that Burn was not hit. Five RPGs hit the vehicles only meters away, but those mechanics kept at it, working forty-five minutes while under direct fire, sometimes crossing fifty meters in the open to relay information.

Men like Burn and Miller who seem completely fearless can be unnerving to enemies. The enemy must have been going crazy trying to shoot them. After forty-five minutes, the mechanics realized the trailer was lost. However, they wanted to save the Land Rover and Saxon, which had been hit by RPGs. Burn got into his unarmored Foden and pulled the death trap around—following an armored Bulldog to a better position—when an IED exploded and killed the Bulldog. Brinkworth moved in with his Warrior to secure the Bulldog whose crew survived with two men injured.

A commander had to tell Burn and Miller that enough was enough; their Foden recovery vehicle needed to be taken off the battlefield. So the REMEs were sent with escort back to Basra Palace. This was Burn's first patrol/combat in Basra. He had been out there for about two hours, and in addition to untold small-arms fire, about twenty RPGs had been fired at the trucks on the bridge. But God smiled on Burn; it's just too bad that nobody back in the UK or USA would likely ever know what the British mechanics in Basra were made of.

Brinkworth, meanwhile, had volunteered to recover the Bulldog. Bullets continued to snap by when Brinkworth climbed out of his hatch and jumped to the street to assess the damage. He could see the recovery would be difficult. The bomb had been well made, and it destroyed a track, making recovery difficult, especially so with all the bullets flying. The only thing standing between Brinkworth and a well-aimed bullet between the eyes were his fellow soldiers returning deadly accurate fire into known and suspected firing positions. Brinkworth somehow got two lines hooked up and dragged the Bulldog back to the Basra Palace.

Yet, all the bullets and bombs were less threatening than the heat. Major James Bryant, commander of R Company 4 Rifles, had been fighting while coordinating the attempted recovery on the bridge. He relieved the platoon at the bridge that had evacuated seven soldiers melting down from the heat.

He parked his Bulldog in a dangerous spot while standing up in his turret to give hand and arm signals to Captain Moger across the canal. *WHAM!!!* Bryant's Bulldog took three RPG hits, but he stayed high to fire his machine gun at the enemy. Although his company took one KIA and eight other casualties, Bryant was still fighting, but running out of ammunition. He'd been lucky so far, and wisely did not push that luck any further. He decided to destroy the damaged vehicles instead of almost certainly losing more soldiers by continuing the recovery efforts. Captain Moger used his last 30mm cannon shots to destroy the vehicles. He had no 30mm and no machine-gun ammo left.

It was time to saddle up and move on. That was 4 Rifles's first trip into Basra—more than fifteen hours of fighting, two killed in action, many wounded, and a convoy of vehicles in various states of damage or destruction.

★   ★   ★

Two days after the ambush, 4 Rifles was back out there. Major Steve Webb, a father of two, led his Welsh Warriors at the point of another convoy. He was just outside of the Basra Palace gate when they were heavily ambushed. The attack, more like a series of ambushes, stretched on for about two and a half miles. Webb's mission was to secure that route for the unarmored resupply convoy. *WhoooshhhBAMMM!!!* An RPG flew nearby over his head, and Webb pointed his Warrior directly into the heaviest fighting. As he and his men fired back at the ambush, *WhoooshhhBAMMM!!!*, another RPG ripped toward them.

The enemy had cracked the code. Wherever the technology originated from, the enemy was now emplacing EFPs to hit the most vulnerable parts of the Warrior. This EFP was dead-on. The molten-copper slug blasted perfectly through the Warrior's weakest area, shattering fragments from the Warrior's own armor into the crew compartment. Color Sergeant Mark Hughes was alive. The lenses of his goggles had blown out, although the frames were still strapped to his head. The deafened soldiers checked each other. Though Hughes's gear was singed and the insides of his legs were slightly burned, he was otherwise OK.

Shrapnel heading for Major Steve Webb missed him by about eight inches, slamming into the batteries and wiping them out, filling the interior with acrid smoke. The explosions caused pounds of moon dust to poof up like an opaque thundercloud inside the vehicle and out. The dust alone is worse than the darkest night, because a light won't work in the dust.

Stunned and blinded by the dust, Webb's turret power was out and he had no comms. Somehow he could hear the Warrior motor running and could feel that the vehicle was still driving. This could be good (as in driving the Warrior out of the kill zone), or bad (as in the driver is dead, but somehow the vehicle is still rumbling around). With comms down, Webb could not contact the driver, PTE David Smith, to find out. In the darkness Webb cocked his rifle and climbed blindly to the top of the vehicle and then down to Smith's hatch. Soldiers in other vehicles could see bullets raining down on Webb's wounded Warrior, as he crouched down—if he fell forward, he'd be flattened like a pancake under the tracks—and yelled at Smith who, luckily enough, was wounded but still alive.

The EFP had missed PTE David Smith by inches, but Smith

had leg wounds and serious burns to his backside. Somehow he managed to press on. While bullets hailed down on the vehicle, Webb clung to part of the armor and stayed with Smith, guiding him forward. Smith, still sitting on burned flesh in the driver's seat, in that searing engine heat under heavy body armor, never told Major Webb how badly he had been burned. Major Webb needed a radio to continue leading the fight, so when another Warrior pulled alongside, he leapt to it, took command, and continued to attack into the ambush, simultaneously organizing Smith's evacuation and the stricken Warrior's recovery. After two and a half hours of fighting, Webb managed to push and pull the convoy through the city. Webb's Warrior had saved his soldiers, but its fuel had leaked out through ruptured tanks, and it had to be towed.

The missions continued. Nearly every patrol got into combat. Often the soldiers would have to clear a dozen or so EFPs just to move through the city, and the price of missing just once could be death by flames. Veritable belts of IEDs were established. People were killed within a quarter mile of the front gate. Over a hundred strikes on vehicles occurred within three months.

Just as this book goes to print, a British officer happened to contact me saying that Major Steve Webb and CPL Adam Miller received awards for valor, which read:

Corporal Adam Miller, Corps of Royal Electrical and Mechanical Engineers, is awarded the Conspicuous Gallantry Cross. In an attempt to recover a military vehicle CPL Miller worked tirelessly for nearly two hours, much of that time under constant and heavy fire in a 360° and three-dimensional urban battle. CPL Miller displayed extraordinary dedication, icy nerve, and determination.

Good grief, CPL Miller's award is understated. The British Army might consider hiring me to write their awards for a little more drama. Then Webb's:

Major Stephen Nicholas WEBB (537535)
The Royal Welsh
Webb had been exposed to enemy fire almost daily with two vehicles destroyed under him by improvised explosive devices. B Company had a casualty rate of almost 15%, including three dead, but under his leadership morale was sky high. He displayed selfless courage, conspicuous gallantry, and inspiring leadership of the very highest order.

Understated again. Must be a Brit thing.

Leaving Basra

The Brits have been involved since the very beginning of the Iraqi nation, when it was created from broken pieces of the Ottoman Empire. British military forces were instrumental in defeating the Ottoman Empire in the Mesopotamian campaign during World War I, losing more than ninety thousand soldiers. T. E. Lawrence helped organize and lead the Arab insurgency against the Turks, skillfully blending Great Game diplomacy and guerilla warfare.

Following the war, Great Britain was given a League of Nations mandate over the new nation of Iraq, where the two regions Baghdad and Basra had been joined together (later the region of Mosul was added, forming Iraq's present-day boundaries). The British restored the Hashemite monarchy and appointed Sunni to major administrative and political positions. In 1932, Iraq was granted independence, although the regime's coziness with the Nazis led the British to invade the country in 1941 and occupy it until 1947. I have seen the old British gravestones in Iraq.

Great Britain played an important role in the 1991 Gulf War, being the second-largest contributor of forces and suffering twenty-four killed in action, nine of whom were killed by friendly fire from the Americans. British forces were in charge of stabilizing Kuwait, once Sadaam's troops were pushed out.

The British name for the current war in Iraq is "Operation Telic," or Op Telic, though practically no British soldiers know what the "Telic" means. (Actually, it means "pertaining to philosophic purpose or end.") Initially, Great Britain was responsible for four southern Iraqi provinces: Muthanna, Dhi Qar, Maysan, and al Basra (of which Basra is the capital). All of these provinces have been returned to provincial Iraqi control (PIC). The lines of influence in the area are largely tribal and sectarian, with most folks being Shia. There is little al Qaeda activity. The Coalition still operates in these provinces, but its role is significantly reduced.

Since the British rotate every six months, the Op Telic number changes every six months. Telic 1 was eventful because it was the invasion. But Telics 2–8 were nearly sleepwalks (with the exception of Telic 4, when nine British soldiers were KIA and thirty-five wounded in a six-month period), and so Basra fell off the map. Shots were rarely fired, and journalists spent relatively little time there. The British were treading water while the Americans sorted out "northern Iraq."

Counterinsurgency experts cautioned Coalition members from the outset that liberators have a limited shelf life, after which they become occupiers. While the American shelf life in some regions was measured in weeks and months, tolerance for the British was being measured in years. But as the war dragged on, the British expiration date in Basra passed; they outlived their welcome in the southern provinces.

By the third month of Telic 10, 4 Rifles soldiers had been hit with about seventeen hundred rockets and mortars at their small encampment at Basra Palace. One day, more than seventy rockets and mortars exploded inside the compound. Just walking to breakfast or lunch could be a deadly mission. Some soldiers ate only once per day. And 4 Rifles fired more than thirty-seven thousand rounds of machine gun and rifle ammunition. They fired grenades, Javelin missiles, and artillery. American jets and helicopters launched rockets and dropped bombs.

In total, Telic 10 sustained twenty-two KIA and one hundred thirty-four wounded in three months. Per capita, that's more intense than the combat our own troops faced. Danger was everywhere. Even sleep proved deadly as mortars and rockets rained into British bases. During one single attack when the PJCC (Provincial Joint Coordination Center, a sort of headquarters for joint Coalition and Iraqi efforts) was nearly overrun, British soldiers fired about twelve thousand five hundred rounds over four hours. Another mission was hit with twenty-three IEDs and thirty-eight RPGs.

The oppressive southern heat accounted for casualties that do not show up in combat statistics. Basra is hotter than most of Iraq, and temperatures inside the armored vehicles could rise to 150° F. During one twelve-hour mission, the Brits took only four wounded to enemy action, but another eighteen to heat.

Unlike Diyala province and other places up north, in Basra instead of civil war there were relatively minor domestic power struggles among tribes, militias, and criminal organizations. In the midsection of Iraq, most of the violence is Iraqis killing Iraqis, which is why we were hated at first (we failed to keep order) and are hailed now (some trusted arbiter has to put a stop to it). In Basra some ninety percent of the attacks were directed against the British. They realized that the best thing they could do for Basra was to remove themselves from the fray.

British forces left their small outpost in Basra Palace on September 2, 2007. Basra province was turned over to provincial Iraqi control on December 15. British Prime Minister Gordon Brown announced that British troops would be drawn down. Some troops would stay to train Iraqi soldiers; the Brits have long trained foreign armies in their former colonies and elsewhere around the world and are very good it. The British combat mission was essentially finished.

The British had not failed. The prognosis for the region was good. Rogue elements in the Basra police had been a huge part of the violence both against the British and Iraqis. As a result, the Baghdad government had taken some three thousand Basra police, shipped them elsewhere in Iraq, and replaced their commander with a more trusted figure, General Mohan. After General Mohan assumed control, Basra police reported a seventy percent drop in crime. I witnessed this change in atmosphere and reported the extent of the calm, countering mainstream media reports that falsely claimed Basra had descended into chaos in the wake of the pull-back.

★   ★   ★

While I was embedded with the British, I asked British soldiers how they were treated back home. They said they were mostly ignored. Occasionally they expressed a muted desire to get the treatment they imagined American soldiers receive. They thought our troops got big parades and hugs from strangers at the airport. To be sure, some do. Our soldiers get care packages from people they do not even know, and those packages are excellent morale boosters. They get cards from kindergartens across the land and paste them on the walls of their headquarters and hospitals. British receive cards and packages like this, but nothing like the ones American soldiers get.

They did tell me about one woman who gives them great moral support. They say she handwrites a letter to every wounded soldier in 4 Rifles and to every family of a soldier who is lost. She writes letters to the battalion. She e-mails Lieutenant Colonel Patrick Sanders, asking how the soldiers are doing. She sends hundred-dollar bottles of Scotch to wounded soldiers in 4 Rifles, and she presented their medals to them when they returned home after their deployment was finished. The soldiers say things like, "She's so busy, yet finds time to handwrite all those letters to our wounded and families." A soldier told me that she even invited the families to her own home.

She is, of course, Her Royal Highness, the Duchess of Cornwall, married to the Prince of Wales, the next King of England. Americans may get parades, but these Brits get invited to the palace.

Tea and Progress

In December 2007, I went home for Christmas, cautiously optimistic about the progress we'd made in a year, with the emphasis on "cautiously."

On January 30, 2008, I landed in Baghdad on a Japanese Air Force flight from Kuwait. I embedded with the 1st Squadron 4th Cavalry. After the 1-4 CAV soldiers picked me up at the airport, I pulled on heavy body armor, and we headed straight into a mission that lasted into the early evening. No drama this time. There wasn't even any radio chatter about any action .

Early in 2007, 1-4 CAV's area of operation (AO) in southern Baghdad was one of the most dangerous in Iraq. In 2008, the same area is safer than the "Green Zone." We walked around and talked with Iraqis for several hours. The Iraqi kids were learning English. The kids came up to the 1-4 CAV soldiers, and the soldiers knew the kids' names, while the kids called the soldiers by their names and ranks. The Iraqi moms in the 1-4 area are encouraging their children to learn our language, and the kids often act as on-the-spot interpreters for their parents or others in their neighborhood.

The 1-4 CAV had not been attacked since September 9, 2007. Almost five months. This was incredible. I remember my first embed with 1-4 CAV in late March 2007. Almost as soon as I arrived, we went out on a raid; the next day we were in a fire fight. Artillery fired over our heads at night. But even then, there were glints of hope that I wrote about. Now those glints are like spotlights.

The neighborhood was a mix of Sunni and Shia. By late 2007 and early 2008, there was so much cooperation between the 1-4 CAV soldiers and their Iraqi neighbors, both Sunni and Shia, the place seemed surreal. That's how bad it had been and how good it was: the reappearance of normal life seemed surreal. The commander LTC James Crider sometimes joked to me that it was going so well that it seemed like *The Truman Show*, and it was true. Those of us who had seen it before (often with ears ringing from machine guns and explosions) were astonished at the civility and progress on the streets. Was this the same Iraq?

Two of the southern Baghdad neighborhoods in the 1-4's Area of Operation were known as Mulhallah 840 and 838. The markets were open and filled with goods for sale. There were working streetlights, playgrounds, Internet cafés, and at least one video-game store where kids played combat games. (Boys will be boys.) The people were hopeful. I liked these neighborhoods, because it was easy to walk around and talk to Iraqis without fear of being attacked. Mulhallah 838 was so safe it felt like Dohuk in the northern Kurdish region, where I spent days alone and unarmed.

The citizens who were finally finding peace were fully enrolled in the effort to keep it. LTC James Crider told me the story of one local bad guy who had been detained but was released, only to return to the neighborhood. Within a day, eleven Iraqis had either called in to the 1-4 CAV tip line, or stopped soldiers on the streets to report the bad guy's presence. I did not witness that incident, but I could write for many pages similar things I have personally witnessed in the 1-4 area. Al Qaeda is trying to regenerate in the area, but the people dime out al Qaeda the moment their little heads hit the sunlight. Al Qaeda will continue to land blows against our Iraqi allies and us, but there will be no caliphate. Al Qaeda has lost Iraq.

The 4th Infantry Brigade Combat Team 1st Infantry Division (4-1 I/D) Dragon Brigade at Forward Operating Base (FOB) Falcon in southern Baghdad is extremely open to the press, and readers of this book have learned that a unit that tries to lasso reporters to write about their efforts probably is ahead of the game on counterinsurgency. At the Dragon Brigade, press can come and stay as long as they wish, and go anywhere they wish to go. Not surprisingly, the Dragon Brigade pulls down more good press than just about anyone in Iraq. Part of this is because of the tiny four-man Public Affairs Office (PAO) staff consisting of one officer and three enlisted: Major Kirk Luedeke from Hudson, NH; Sergeant First Class Robert Timmons from Menifee, CA; Corporal Ben Washburn from Wilmington, NC; and Specialist Nathaniel Smith from Round Rock, TX.

These four soldiers, who call themselves "The Ghostwriters," would hardly be noticed in a gun-centric environment. They were worth a thousand rifles in the counterinsurgency. They do their best to drag the press down here, and they have a good story to tell. General Petraeus told me in July 2007 that southern Baghdad was the canary in the mineshaft. Major Kirk Luedeke, the commander of the Ghostwriters, provided me the following facts to chart the progress in the Rashid district of southern Baghdad. The canary is doing pretty well:

In January 2007, there were 553 bodies found in Rashid District killed by sectarian violence.

In January 2008, there were 16.

In January 2007, there were 33 rocket or mortar attacks.

In January 2008, there were 7.

In January 2007, there were 113 direct fire attacks against Coalition or Iraqi Security Forces.

In January 2008, there were 45.

In January 2007, there were 184 IEDs.

January 2008, there were 51.

In January 2007, the total number of enemy-initiated events was 883.

In January 2008, there were only 119.

The small PAO staff at the Dragon Brigade was dominating its media battle space; al Qaeda's media arm didn't have a chance in 4-1's area of operations. Morale in the Ghostwriters' office was higher than in any PAO office I had seen. They knew they were making a difference. They were unappreciated, I believe, but the soldiers of 4-1 should know that all the good press lavished on them was facilitated by the Ghostwriters.

On February 1, I went with LTC Crider to a lunch with sheiks and other Iraqi leaders. We arrived at an older sheik's spacious home sitting amid the squalor that has engulfed most of Baghdad. Less than five minutes later, giant MRAPs (mine resistant armor protected vehicles) came rumbling down the road, pausing to push up wires along the way so as not to rip them out of the houses.

An MRAP ramp dropped, and down climbed Colonel Rick Gibbs, commander of the Dragon Brigade. The old sheik met us at the front gate, warmly greeting COL Gibbs and LTC Crider, and we all stepped inside the two-story home. It was clean and comfortable, and well decorated in Iraqi fashion, with antique swords on the wall and a rifle that might have been a hundred years old. Had the sheik's great grandfather toted that rifle while riding a camel into battle? The big carpets under our feet looked like they might be from Iran, but the old sheik said they came from Germany. So much for ambience and flying carpets and genies emerging from teapots.

There was a huge table of food, enough to feed at least fifty men. Bananas, apples, oranges, and other fruits on one end, along with cans of Pepsi, bottles of Coke, 7UP, orange soft drinks, and bottled water, all arranged in rows on the table. Baked chicken, beef, rice, many types of vegetables, all smelled sumptuous, but they were still cooking in the kitchen. I was ready to eat right then. But it was just before noon, and little did I know that we had ninety minutes of talk between us and that food.

The conversation began. The interpreter used to be Iraqi, but he moved to America years ago and is an American now. His name is Edward, and Edward has spent an incredible four years doing combat interpreting, mostly in southern Baghdad. (It's a wonder he's still alive; interpreter has been one of the most dangerous jobs in Iraq.) Edward is an excellent interpreter, and the soldiers admire Edward's courage.

The old sheik, who seemed upset, asked, "Where is Captain Cook?" The Iraqis I've met treat CPT Cook like a local sheik. The kids knew his name. ("Hey Captain Cook!" "Hey Mohammed!") When LTC Crider replied that Captain Cook was on the way, the old sheik smiled as if hearing that his favorite grandson was coming after all.

By 12:15, we had shed our helmets and body armor, and once we finished with all the formalities of hugs-and-kisses-and-we-all-love-each-other, we sat on comfortable couches. There were six Iraqi men and the old sheik, five American soldiers, plus Edward.

At first the talk was higher level, with Colonel Gibbs explaining a few things about money for Iraq being delayed in

America. Colonel Gibbs said that he had spent about $180 million in the area, but that new funds were being held up by politics in Washington.

After some conversation, the old sheik saw that I was taking notes. Through Edward, he told me the problems of the Sunni and Shia did not exist before the invasion but were created when a few traitorous Iraqis gave President Bush bad advice, which the Iranians then exploited.

"The Iranians are poison to the Iraqi people," said the old sheik.

The sheik explained he was from the Jabouri tribe and that many Jabouri are Sunni, like him, but many others are Shia. He pointed to someone across the room and said, "That is my son-in-law, and he is Shia!" and his son-in-law smiled. The fabric of Iraq is finely woven. The old sheik said that friends who often came to his house were both Sunni and Shia and even prayed together. Most of the Shia in his neighborhood had been "cleansed" by al Qaeda, which upset the old Sunni sheik. He wants his Shia neighbors to come back.

At 12:35, when Captain Cook finally arrived, the old sheik stood briskly to meet him, and they met with the handshake/hug that is normal, but warmer than usual, like a grandfather meets a grandson. Now that Captain Cook was there, Colonel Gibbs mostly just sat back and listened to Cook and the old sheik talk. Meanwhile, the old sheik and Captain Cook were arguing nearly constantly, and Cook was saying the old sheik was wrong about this or that. Later I mentioned to Captain Cook how strange it was that the sheik seemed upset when Cook was not there, but then when he finally arrived, the two of them spent most of the time arguing about neighborhood business. Cook said they argued all the time, and often it was much worse.

The talk rambled on until 12:55, when another group of Iraqis arrived. General Kareem from the National Police came in wearing a brown leather jacket, along with two other NP commanders in their uniforms. There was an Iraqi lieutenant colonel from the 3-1-3 Iraqi Army along with his American counterpart LTC Watson and three more sheiks. I inventoried the room and counted twenty-three men, but the room would have comfortably absorbed thirty.

The old sheik and another sheik were thumbing their prayer beads as the conversation rambled over important topics. The old sheik began complaining again that he wanted his Shia friends to move back into their homes and that none were coming. Captain Cook said that thirty or forty or even fifty Shia families had already moved back, but the sheik kept saying none were coming back and Cook kept saying, "Yes, they are coming back! I can show you." They could have been married.

At 1325 hours, the old sheik declared it was time to eat, and so we ate with our bare hands while standing at the long table. The food was delicious, and Colonel Gibbs said that when he goes home, he'll have to relearn to eat with fork and spoon. General Kareem chuckled. And then General Kareem asked Gibbs which tribe he planned to register for? "Al Ameriki" tribe, he said. Kareem laughed, and they kept talking.

The lunch over, we lined up to wash our hands, and it was time to go. I asked to ride back in Colonel Gibbs's MRAP. On the way back, we stopped at a park that was under construction but had been stalled because the American funds had dried up. As we were riding in the back of the MRAP, talking over the headsets, Edward told me about an incident that happened in Arab Jabour about three weeks prior. More than thirty al Qaeda had kicked an old lady and her family out of their home. The old woman did what a lot of Iraqis do: she called the Americans. Edward was one of the Americans, and she gave Edward the exact location of the house, which the Americans confirmed before dropping a bomb on it and killing more than thirty al Qaeda. The Americans then began the process of paying for the house.

That same day, on February 1, 2008, in the al Ghazl market in another part of Baghdad, al Qaeda sent two mentally disabled women into two crowded pet markets as suicide bombers. The explosions killed more than ninety Iraqis.

On the day of the meeting at the sheik's house in southern Baghdad, there was some drama between the National Police (NP) and the concerned local citizens group, who were now called the "Sons of Iraq." Technically, the Sons of Iraq (SOI) in southern Baghdad work for the National Police (NP), but they are paid by the Coalition. This was a temporary and politically expedient compromise given the friction between the SOI and the Iraqi police. The Iraqi government was blocking SOI members from joining the police force. Meanwhile, many Sunni neighborhoods in Baghdad could be guarded only by the SOI, since the mostly Shia NP are often corrupt and unprofessional, some of them members of death squads. In early 2007, a bunch of police in Baghdad openly joked with me that they were members of JAM.

While we had been at the sheik's for lunch, an NP reportedly insulted some SOI, apparently referring to their women. The SOI swarmed toward the NP. Luckily, General Kareem from the NP came out and calmed everyone down, just before heading over to the lunch.

After lunch, I drove off with Colonel Ricky Gibbs in his MRAP, leaving 1-4 CAV behind in Mulhallah 840. While we drove away, about thirty SOI carrying AK-47s confronted the NPs. Soldiers from the 1-4 CAV intervened to calm things down, but the SOI were too agitated. The American soldiers made the decision to take all of their weapons—the SOI gave them up voluntarily, a feat that could only be accomplished from a position of great trust and moral high ground. Other members of SOI were observed by 1-4 CAV soldiers apparently setting an ambush for the NPs, but the soldiers intervened and stopped that potential catastrophe as well. No shots fired. Our guys told the NPs to go home for the day, and they did, another feat that could only be accomplished from respect, trust, and high ground. The American soldiers returned the SOI their weapons without ammunition.

The next day, we had a meeting with eight Iraqis, five men from the neighborhoods, and three junior NP officers to discuss the distribution of thirty-six thousand liters of kerosene that, after much aggressive lobbying from the Americans, the Iraqi government had finally agreed to hand over to the neighborhood. After the kerosene chat, LTC Crider brought up yesterday's narrowly averted bloodbath between the NPs and Sons of Iraq and how the stupid remarks of one NP could have led to a shootout. Crider calmly talked about the importance of professionalism. At first the conversation between the Iraqis was civil, but soon voices were rising and hands were flying. Crider just listened for a while and then intervened saying simply: "Be calm. I am calm."

And that was it. Like the Horse Whisperer.

The Iraqis calmed down immediately. Crider said not to punish the NP who had committed the insult. The Iraqis who had seemed ready to bury the NP alive, suddenly were fine with just using it as a lesson. No punishment. Just move on. After the meeting, we went back into the Humvees and drove out to the neighborhoods.

We walked around and talked with folks for a couple hours, including the Sons of Iraq with their AK-47s. The SOI we spoke with did not want to fight the NPs. But they were guarding their neighborhoods, and would not hesitate to flat-blast a truckload of NPs if they came around abusing people. Originally, the neighborhoods were a mix of Sunni and Shia, although many Shia moved out when it got too dangerous. Now that the neighbor-hoods were peaceful, the Shia were moving back in. The Sunni SOI protect the Shia too.

While we walked around, there were many "thank yous" and smiles from the locals; lots of complaints too. The 1-4 CAV was the de-facto government for Mulhallah 838 and Mulhallah 840. At one point, Crider was surrounded by some fifteen men com-plaining about the government of Iraq, saying it was useless and the Americans ought to whip it into shape.

Captain Cook was responsible for Mulhallah 840. The people of the neighborhood offered Cook a home if he would come back after his deployment ended. I believed they meant it. They would take him in, in exchange for his leadership, but of course he would probably spend most of his time arguing with the old sheik. The Iraqis in Mulhallah 840 wanted President Bush to know they think the government of Iraq is worthless. Interestingly, although they complain about the mostly Shia government, they did not com-plain about the Shia people. They did, however, complain about JAM and asked that the Coalition break the militias.

Iran seems to be a great psychological release valve for Sunni and many Shia. It seems that everything bad the Shia do to the Sunni, the Sunni blame on influence from Iran. If only the Persians would stop making the Shia do bad things. They hate the Iranians with great passion and want to help us attack Iran. Of course I have heard no American soldiers volunteering to invade Iran. The soldiers usu-ally just listen to the Iraqis rail on about Iran until the Iraqis are ex-hausted and complain about something else, but never with the passion that they save for Iran. One minute you are talking to a per-fectly rational Iraqi, who might have perfectly rational complaints about the sorry Iraqi government, and then Iran somehow enters the conversation, and the Iraqis lose their minds and start blaming every-thing from al Qaeda to JAM to global warming on Iran.

Despite various complaints—and the obligatory insults toward Iran—the residents were visibly happy to see us. Both the NPs (who, because they are mostly Shia, the Sunni think are under the spell of Iran) and the SOI were on good behavior. Today was cool, sunny, and bright, and the kids were playing in the playgrounds.

Many writers who come here and see peace, find it boring, and quickly leave in search of action. This was my third trip to visit the 1-4 CAV, and I found talking with Iraqis as peace finally came to them after so much war to be a great thing. Plus it was a good excuse to write about a place where I was not getting shot at all the time. I could study counterinsurgency where it was working and not get shot at, all while events were still very fresh in the minds of the soldiers and the people.

We headed to Mulhallah 838 to see Dr. Mouyad Muslah Hamid al-Jabouri, a cardiologist who had had a prominent medical post in the old regime. Dr. Mouyad operated on one of Saddam's sons after he got shot, plus his mom is a very good cook, so he's great to visit. That Dr. Mouyad had worked on Uday meant that he must have been one of the best doctors in Iraq. When the Americans started spanking al Qaeda in the individual neighborhoods, our folks never knew Dr. Mouyad was there. Beginning about six months ago, Dr. Mouyad emerged from obscurity to become a community leader, helping to renovate the two neighborhoods, both with American money and his own.

Dr. Mouyad could speak intelligently on subjects ranging from sewerage to electricity to tribal matters to high-level Iraqi politics. LTC Crider spent endless hours with the doctor trying to decipher Iraq and to improve the neighborhoods. Talking with Dr. Mouyad for an hour—and we talked many times for many hours—I could learn more about Iraq than I usually learned in days.

So much went on in Dr. Mouyad's home that I called it "The Embassy." Captain Hamilton from the 1-4 CAV had an office there. Battles used to rage so close to Mouyad's home that in 2007, a 1-4 CAV soldier was killed less than fifty meters away from his front gate.

On February 2, 2008, Colonel Gibbs presented Dr. Mouyad with a plaque of appreciation signed by General Petraeus. The same day he received the plaque, Dr. Mouyad was expecting five distinguished visitors from America. Waiting for the visitors to arrive, we discussed a range of issues, including the NP and the knucklehead things they still do. Recently, a resident of Mulhallah 838 had driven up to the checkpoint at the entrance to the neighborhood, and an NP wanted to search his car. There was an argument and the man stepped out. The NP got angry and shot three bullets into the car's engine, ruining it.

How to handle this? Complaining to the NPs would probably achieve little. There is no internal NP mechanism to resolve such conflicts. This was as a tribal matter. The tribe the NP belonged to negotiated with the tribe of the victim and agreed that if the man sold his car, the policeman's tribe would pay the difference between the sale price and the car's value before it was shot. However, the man wanted more than the tribe offered, so the dispute remained open with a lot of interesting drama. Of course, Iraq has government courts, but their rulings are not as respected as tribal settlements.

Though Iraqis know we were torturing Iraqi prisoners earlier in the war, overwhelmingly they accept that we have straightened up and that Americans now treat prisoners very well, typically much better than the Iraqi Government, which, I very strongly believe, still tortures prisoners. Many times I have seen Iraqis come to American commanders asking about a family member or friend who was detained. If they learned the person was detained by

Americans, the Iraqis were relieved. But when they find that a loved one is in Iraqi government custody, there is dread and despair.

Colonel Gibbs told the story of an Iraqi man who turned in his own two sons to Gibbs's Dragon Brigade. The man said he knew if the sons were guilty they would be held, but if innocent would be released. Following an investigation, the Americans kept one son and released the other. Smart father. It's better to be in an American detention facility than have Special Forces blasting down your door.

I stayed with Captain Hamilton, LTC Crider, and others at Dr. Mouyad's house where we talked into the night. Mouyad was full of interesting quotes like: "When you marry without love, it's perfect," and "When a woman knows you love her, she goes crazy." I have this great idea for a book: *Tuesdays with Mouyad*.

I walked down a road—wearing no body armor or helmet—where just seven or eight months previously tanks and Strykers would have been in great danger. Despite the signs of progress, the importance of keeping money flowing to local commanders cannot be understated. Money is ammunition in a counterinsurgency, and commanders have learned to use it effectively at local levels. They say it is better to open schools, build sidewalks, and clean up soccer fields than to buy tanks or lethal weapons. They say this all the time. And it's clear they are speaking the truth.

On February 15, 2007, I left southern Baghdad and flew via a couple of helicopter hops to Mosul. Along the way, we often flew so low over farms that I could smell herds of sheep. Over one stretch, someone had used a tractor to draw a big heart in a field, and then close by, another big heart with an arrow through it. I wondered what that was all about until it hit me. The day before had been Valentine's Day.

CHAPTER SEVENTEEN

Brother Nations

Before patrols leave the gates, soldiers test fire various sorts of machine guns. Each model has a different voice: The little 5.56mm "SAW" machine gun snaps out a hurricane of little bullets; the more powerful 7.62mm medium machine gun can rip a man to pieces, and its bark is deeper and louder than the little hurricane; and finally, the devastating M2 .50-caliber machine gun, called the "Ma Deuce" or "fifty," that is mounted on many Humvees, tanks, and other vehicles and has been outfitted on and used against aircraft. The fifty booms away and can shoot a man in half or a jet out of the sky. Cars often burst into flames when the fifty shreds through. The M2 was designed for World War I, but barely missed that war, finding itself in Audie Murphy's hands in World War II. The fifty has been in the American arsenal for more than eighty years and has hardly changed. And now, as we go into the fifth year of this war, at least a hundred machine guns can be heard test firing every day, out of this single gate, before the soldiers rumble out into

Mosul, to which I returned again in February 2008. Last night while I talked on my satellite phone, I watched a firefight just near base, tracers sometimes arching into the sky. Five years at war in a single city. What have we learned?

On the morning of February 16, at about 3:10 A.M., a concussion roused me from slumber. The blast was so large that I half-expected to find body parts nearby or the wounded screaming or moaning. Such events have happened many times on this base. I rolled from bed already fully dressed, flipped on the red headlamp that I keep around my neck while I sleep, pulled on a pair of shoes, and flipped off the red light while grabbing the night-vision monocular. Stepping into the darkness, a shiver rippled through from the cold. Darkness. My thumb and index finger pulled out and twisted the switch on the night-vision monocular. I peered into the green glow, scanning for a mushroom cloud or flickering brightness, but no fire or radiance appeared in the tube. Back to bed.

There are so many large explosions here that one seldom ventures forth to look, but that blast was peculiar. An officer said later that the explosion had come from a truck bomb containing about five thousand pounds of explosives. It had been captured in Mosul only hours before on February 15 and was taken out of the city and detonated. Less than a month ago, just a few miles from base here in Mosul, an estimated thirty thousand pounds of explosives detonated, killing dozens of Iraqis. The next day, when a police chief came to investigate, he was pelted with rocks and then murdered by a suicide bomber.

On average, every American mission that leaves this base encounters some sort of action. But though the violence seems very high, it is low by comparison to what I witnessed in Mosul during 2005 and 2007. Nevertheless, the approximate thirty thousand-pound detonation and the five thousand-pound detonation, along with hundreds of other recent attacks, indicate an enemy that is ready for us. The terrorists in Iraq, most of them now in this city, are among the "best" in the world, regularly staging complex attacks as deadly and intricate as those depicted in the movie *The Kingdom*. The film, starring Jamie Foxx, was highly dramatized, but the portrayal of the actual attack was par. The five thousand-pound truck bomb that was captured likely would have been followed by other car bombs and other attacks on rescuers. Happens all the time.

Many explosions, day after day. On February 20, a "blackout" has been placed on non-essential Internet and telephone communications. Cables literally were pulled from their sockets, shutting off communications. By now many friends and loved ones of soldiers fighting here will have noticed that communications from soldiers in Mosul abruptly ceased without saying "goodbye." Phone calls ended abruptly. Members of Family Readiness Groups (FRG) will have picked up their phones to call other FRG members, asking if they have heard anything from Mosul. Within an hour, perhaps hundreds of people will figure out that someone in Mosul has been killed. The families, too, are veterans.

The blackout: How many soldiers have died this time? Who was it? By now the commander will have called his own wife, telling her what has happened, and that she must be ready to do her duty as the wife of the commander and for those who will now go forward into forever without their soldier, their father, their son, daughter, or mother. Some wives will sit by the window wondering if the car will park in their driveway, if the men in uniforms will step out, along with the chaplain and the commander's wife.

On February 20, one soldier was killed and three injured in an RPG attack here. Four other soldiers killed in action elsewhere in Iraq are pending identification. Names of the four killed have not yet been released, though journalists who were here sent out blurbs. About four thousand Americans have died in the war, though I already hear grumblings on the Right saying this was not even a "war," but a "conflict." Repackaging the Iraq War as a skirmish dishonors those who fought here.

The same people denied the insurgency and later the civil war in Iraq and the catastrophe unfolding today in Afghanistan. All news organizations, from the newbie blogger to the *New York Times*, from right-wing talk radio to NPR, from CNN to Fox, all ultimately depend upon the financial support of their audiences. So readers and listeners and viewers should not be surprised when media organizations tell them what they want to hear. Happy news for the Left was that U.S. soldiers were demoralized and the war was being lost. Happy news for the Right was that there was no insurgency, then no civil war; we always had enough troops, and we were winning hands-down, except for the left-wing lunatics who were trying to unravel it all. They say heroin addicts are happy, too, when they are out of touch with reality.

During clear mornings, the mountains to the north of Mosul stand white-capped and mysterious, even though I have been there. Lots of Christians live up in that area and they make good food and are welcoming. Some nights the temperature drops below freezing. At 1:30 A.M., on another February night, I stood shivering outside, bathed in bright moonlight on the hill at FOB Marez, and delivered the latest live report from Mosul. There had been explosions earlier, but I saw only lights and stars and the perimeter nearby. Oftentimes the tracer bullets would arc into the sky over Mosul, burn hotly and brightly for a few seconds, and then fall back to Earth and cool, but tonight I saw no tracers.

Most nights there are the buzzing sounds of unmanned spy planes called Shadows launching from their catapults; the invisible Predators are up there, with AirScan doing its thing, the occasional thunder of low-flying jets—and the roar of roof-scraping helicopters, often with the red cross on white background signaling they are medevacs—not that the enemy cares. Throughout day and night, dozens of American patrols drive off base and straight into the city. A handful drive Strykers on special tasks, but most rumble in powerful M1 tanks that the enemy can easily destroy, armored Bradley Fighting Vehicle Systems (BFVS), and armored Humvees that are often swatted off the roads by powerful bombs.

As these words were written, a tremendous explosion rocked the base. I walked out and saw the gigantic mushroom cloud rising. A police station had just been flattened. The morning was blue and cloudless and Rick Tomkins from UPI was out there smoking a cigarette with a cup of coffee. The mushroom cloud rose and slowly traveled what appeared to be southwest, more or less in our direction. The ensuing black smoke from the fire, lower, drifted to the northeast. There was a gunfight, or what sounded like several gunfights, from several directions to the northeast, north, and northwest. The Kiowas were up and looked like gnats next to the mushroom. Armored vehicles rolled out. A suicide truck bomb had attacked the 10 West Police Station, killing at least five, wounding nearly fifty, but by the sound and size of the bomb it could have been two hundred killed. Hard to tell just from the sound. A relatively small bomb often kills many dozens, and then a gigantic bomb sometimes kills nobody. Sometimes there are sharp firefights with thousands of rounds fired, yet nobody gets a scratch, or a small burst that can last seconds at most, and several men die.

★　　★　　★

We are hobbled now in Mosul by having too few troops in Iraq, even while the debate continues to swirl at home about troop reductions. That we are in 2008 running counterinsurgency operations from tanks or Bradleys is a clear sign that we do not have enough paint to cover this barn. Running a counterinsurgency from an M1 tank or a Bradley is like running a bakery from a Bradley. This is not a "kinetic" fight here, yet I see tanks rolling out on patrol day and night. Five years into the war and we are patrolling Mosul—in a counterinsurgency fight—with tanks! We need infantry. We do not have enough. The commanders know we need more soldiers. Petraeus and his staff are experts at counterinsurgency. They are doing the best they can with what they were given, but that the Iraqis and the Coalition have turned this war around in 2007 and 2008 never having the resources they needed is miraculous.

I asked a major in the 3-3 ACR why his soldiers are not outfitted for counterinsurgency, and he replied that they are not doing any counterinsurgency, but that *the sum* of their actions, along with that of the Iraqi Army and Police and the Provincial Reconstruction Team, *in total*, amounted to counterinsurgency. If he believed that, he was clueless. If he thought I believed that, he was wrong.

But though we have a skeleton crew in Mosul with the wrong type of gear for counterinsurgency, we are now beginning to reap the benefits of the last few years of building up the Iraqi security forces under Casey and Petraeus: the Iraqi Army and Iraqi Police are taking the lead in Mosul. This fight is now mostly theirs, though they are lacking many essentials; they do not have enough vehicles. The Iraqi Police and Iraqi Army here are incredibly brave. They keep fighting and are getting better, but they are not ready yet to go it alone.

★   ★   ★

It is fitting that the final words of this book are being written in Mosul, the city that in 2003 showed so much promise as a model for post-Saddam Iraq, thanks to the leadership of General

Petraeus and the Screaming Eagles of the 101st Airborne. The people of Mosul remember those days, five long years ago, and even today many long for the return of the 101st. Most people remember only commanders who fail spectacularly, or spectacularly succeed. In Mosul they know the name Petraeus.

Throughout 2005, the Iraqi Army and Iraqi Police in Mosul improved month by month, and recruits would form long lines to volunteer. Here's one sign: the Iraqis took much heavier losses than we did, but their morale seemed to improve. Iraqi forces that used to flee would now stand and fight, partly because their American trainers would stand and fight with them. The Iraqis were amazed that American officers and sergeants would lead from the front into the worst situations. This even caused some friction during 2005. I recall CPT Matt McGrew, who lived and fought with Iraqis, talking about how some Iraqi officers became upset with American leaders during the early days, because in the Iraqi view officers were not supposed to be leading from the front. Seeing how American officers and sergeants behaved, the Iraqi jundis (soldiers) began to hold their own leaders in contempt. Iraqi soldiers might be a lot of things, but cowards they are not. Before this war some said personal courage was passé in a high-tech war. But we have learned that moral and physical courage are as essential now as ever. Soon the Iraqi officers who survived and mattered were leading from the front. Courage is not in short supply in Iraq.

Leading the Iraqis by example worked, but cost us casualties. The American combat soldiers I was within Mosul in 2005 were not there to play it safe. Their goal was to win. If it cost blood, then blood it would cost. The Iraqis were wild for that sort of leadership.

If a soldier goes to war with the primary goal of returning home alive and in once piece, he does not go to win. An enemy who senses his opponent is not willing to die to kill him gains a supreme advantage. The enemies here have been courageous and tough, but our folks and the Iraqi forces were too formidable, and the enemy learned that our people and the Iraqi forces would close in and kill them if they dared stand their ground. This is important: an enemy forced to choose between dying or hiding inevitably loses legitimacy. Legitimacy is essential. Men who must always either run or die are no longer an army and are not going to found a caliphate. They are just a gang, no matter how brave, and though a gang may frighten and coerce the people, it cannot win the people.

We are not impressed by their suicide bombers. Deadly, yes, but they are merely using programmable humans as low-tech guidance systems. They are the cult version of smart bombs, but they signal desperation and fanaticism, not invincibility.

By the end of 2005, we had killed off key pieces of the insurgency in Mosul, while we put another queen on the chessboard here in the form of amazing progress of the Iraqi security forces. We had achieved so much that our progress was often overstated. During late 2005 or early 2006, a respected veteran commander mentioned to me that the battle for Mosul had been won. I changed the subject. It was not over. And in some ways the war was just getting started in the rest of Iraq. Violence countrywide would peak in 2006 when the civil war hit apogee. Al Qaeda itself, the sheiks, the surge, and our own increasing proficiency with counterinsurgency would give us our second chance. And so our very success has brought us back here to Mosul where we began to win the peace in 2003 and then began to lose it.

Mosul is where some people without understanding are saying we are about to fight the final battle.

The final battle. That would be a good dramatic end for this book and this war. But in a successful counterinsurgency, there are no final battles. No Appomattox Courthouse. No bunker in Berlin.

Not even a Yorktown. "Final battles" can happen when the insurgents win, as Cornwallis discovered. Even then, sometimes the final "battle" is just the helicopter lifting the last one off from the embassy roof.

Nevertheless, what is happening here in Mosul is important. Al Qaeda is being ripped out by the hair and roots; make no mistake about that, but this will take a long time.

American brass has been saying, "al Qaeda in Iraq cannot win without Baghdad, but they cannot survive without Mosul." And if we—and "we" these days means the Iraqi Army and Police as much as anything—can take al Qaeda and the other relatively small coteries of true death-loving fanatics among the insurgents off the board, the only people left on the "other" side will be people it is possible to talk to, and people with whom deals can be made, and with peace we can begin to come home.

Yet the same factors that make Mosul the main place al Qaeda has gone to ground make it a difficult place from which to root them out. This is not Baqubah, a city al Qaeda nearly owned and therefore a city that could be taken away from them, block by deadly block. Mosul is a city they hide in because they know they can. This place is nearly ten times bigger than Baqubah, and we have a small fraction of American troops here compared to what we had for Arrowhead Ripper. Truly, Mosul will mostly be done by the Iraqis, a great test for our allies.

Mosul is the last major terrorist holdout in Iraq. But in Mosul that means something very different than in most of rest of the country. In Mosul the terrorists make up a super-amalgam of groups, some of which are so abstruse and amorphous that it's almost worthless to try to learn their names unless you are an intelligence officer. Trying to keep track is like venturing into your backyard and trying to remember all the bugs' names. At first there seem to be only a few: dragonflies (1920s), cockroaches (al Qaeda), another type of cockroach (Ansar al Sunna), dung beetles (Islamic State of Iraq [ISI]). But if you get down on your hands and knees and part the grass, a whole new world unfolds down there. Insects you never knew existed, lots of varieties, a few main groups, lots of overlap, sometimes cooperating and sometimes ratting each other out to us for business reasons: the gangs infringe on each other's rackets. Even a manicured yard is a little jungle, and Mosul is not little, nor is it manicured.

Mosul is awash in money, at least by Iraqi standards, and it is a trade crossroads for weapons and other commodities. Terrorists sometimes come up from Baghdad to get better prices here. Mosul provides many sources of income for the groups, sources of the sort that encourage rivalry rather than cooperation. Kidnapping is an old standby. A Chaldean archbishop was kidnapped February 29 in Mosul, and the ransom has been raised more than once. Pope Benedict XVI has complained from Rome. But these kidnappers are sure the Vatican is flush with cash too. Is this about religion, or just business? Even if the Vatican does not do a secret payoff, local Christians are known to have money. In February, one of the platoons here happened to rescue a Christian man who was being "stored" underground. Our guys found him by accident. (Accidental rescues happen frequently. Some of the accidental rescues have a *Silence of the Lambs* feel; the hostages often are stored underground for long periods.) The going price for ransom used to be about $50K, and I think that's still about right, but an archbishop has to be worth a lot more than that.

The black market in fuel is another source of terrorist income. Bureaucratic niceties that we take for granted in the West, such as title registries to verify who owns a piece of real estate, are unreliable or non-existent here. So there is a racket in forging deeds and then extorting payments from the real owners. And there is the straight old protection racket.

Then there is the Saudi Connection. More Saudis have been getting caught and killed here recently, and well-placed sources tell me money is "apparently" flowing in from Saudi Arabia and probably to folks like al Qaeda.

So money, as well as differences about the ultimate objective (destroy the West, destroy Iraq, reclaim Iraq for Iraqis, keep the rackets going), tend to leave the insurgencies fractured in Mosul. They have more reason to fight than to cooperate. On the west side of Mosul, lots of the bad guys come from places like Tal Afar. In the east, they tend to be Mosul natives. The mostly Turkomen bad guys from Tal Afar don't mix easily with some Arab terrorist groups, nor Kurdish ones.

When terrorists flee from places like Ramadi and Fallujah (the two biggest cities in Anbar), they naturally go to places like Baqubah (they lost), Baghdad (they lost), and Mosul (here we go), whose diversity has two advantages: it's easier to hide, and if your goal, like al Qaeda's, is to start a civil war, it's easier to start an argument. They don't go to places like Basra or Erbil, where Iraqis will squash al Qaeda faster than the roaches can breed.

The Anbar Awakening began in 2006, many months before "the surge" was in place and was already driving al Qaeda out of Anbar and into places like Baghdad, Arab Jabour, Baqubah, and Mosul. So even if there had never been a surge, the Awakening would have driven terrorists to Mosul. When I was in Mosul in January 2007, al Qaeda already was coming into the city in higher numbers. They tried to overrun a police station, for instance, with a very well-coordinated complex attack that lasted several hours. The serious al Qaeda influx has been happening for more than a year.

Yet the diversity of groups operating in Mosul meant that al Qaeda never controlled Mosul the way they controlled Baqubah and so many places in Anbar. In Baqubah it was easy to follow the plot: first the 1920s and AQI were allies against us (and the JAM also had influence, mostly in reaction to 1920s and al Qaeda); then when AQI revealed its true colors, the 1920s started fighting AQI with mixed success; and then out of necessity the 1920s joined with us to wipe out al Qaeda. That fight was fairly easy to understand. In Mosul, things are never so simple.

The hatred al Qaeda earned was our greatest advantage in the Iraqi midsection, winning us allies among the sheiks and pro-Iraq insurgent groups like the 1920s. In Mosul, the small group of 1920s up here, vestigial appendages of Saddam's reign, remain against us. We have zero Sons of Iraq (or Concerned Local Citizens [CLCs]) in Mosul, and the population does not necessarily rank security at the top of their list of desires. Electricity and jobs seem to be higher on the list. The local people are not convulsing to vomit out AQI as they did in Anbar and Baqubah. All this, along with simply not having enough troops, means there simply will not be a decisive battle with the conditions at hand.

General Petraeus has pointed out for a long time that there is no purely military solution to the fighting in Iraq. The goal now is to identify and isolate the intractable players like al Qaeda and then to kill, capture, fracture, demoralize, or otherwise render them ineffective. Everyone else we want to talk with, not shoot.

Jaysh al-Mahdi is the most powerful umbrella in Iraq, but it is not intractable like AQI. JAM's growth was largely a response to groups attacking Shia, such as AQI (and us crushing Fallujah twice, torturing people at Abu Ghraib, and other such activities). Much of the JAM leadership can be brought to the table to talk politics. Like JAM, most other players seem prone to making more or less rational decisions. And though they do bad things, they also respond to pain and compliance and rewards, whereas the AQI cadre generally needs to be killed. The rational parties make up most of the folks still carrying guns, and most of them have zero "jihad" going. They are after worldly things: money, power, security. Motivations we understand intimately.

★   ★   ★

So Mosul is complicated, and it will take a while. But after five years of blood, toil, and mountains of treasure, Iraq is coming into brighter days. Violence is down. Iraqis who previously wanted dollars when I shopped in their stores now prefer to be paid in Iraqi dinar. The civil war has ended. People are coming home. People say, "Thank you, thank you, thank you."

Iraq is one nation. Those who suggest that Iraq should be partitioned, noting Iraqis often do not get along and the Sunni-Shia rift is profound, miss the crucial reality that Iraqis consider themselves foremost to be Iraqis. The conflicts between Iraqi Sunni and Shia are largely political, not theological. Al Qaeda, now the main instigator of civil war, is thoroughly discredited and strategically crushed in Iraq. Today, al Qaeda's attempts to incite sectarian violence only backfire.

Iraqis are willing to fight for Iraq.

A good deal of this war was American soldiers and Iraqis sitting together, drinking tea, and working out problems like businesspeople. Religion rarely came up in these meetings. Just because Iraqis have "Allahu Akbar" on their flag doesn't mean they're going to blow up the World Trade Center any more than "In God We Trust" means we're going to attack Communist China.

Iraq does not hate America. If they hated us, I'd be urging an immediate troop withdrawal, because there would be no hope of winning this war. If the Iraqis hated us, we would be fighting the Iraqi Police and the Iraqi Army. Instead, we're fighting alongside them.

Several times I have told Iraqis, "One day Iraq and America

can be good friends." They look at me in disbelief. "What do you mean?" they say. "We already are good friends."

At this point no nation on Earth knows more about Iraq than the United States. Iraqis have an affinity for things American. You see it everywhere. There's a gym in the Dora neighborhood of southern Baghdad named "Arnold Gym." Arnold Gym is little more than a bench and a few free weights, but the kids who work out there not only admire the governor of California, whom they have never met, but also the American soldiers whom they see every day. In Mosul in 2007, Command Sergeant Major James Pippin taught the local children to raise their index fingers and pinkies and say, "Hook 'em horns." The kids had no idea what that meant, and neither did I, but they did it every time a Humvee passed because they respected CSM Pippin, who got shot, then mostly healed up after many painful months, and returned to the battle.

There are lots of kitchen accidents in Iraq. Kids get burned. American soldiers can't take it when they see a kid get burned. If they are in the neighborhood on a mission and they see a burned kid, they will cancel the mission to get the kid to an American aid station, which, technically, they shouldn't be doing. But a lot of tough soldiers get weak knee'd when they see a kid in trouble. They'll shoot insurgents all day and all night and can't get enough of it, but when they see a kid hurt, they'll stop and drive off with the kid. Thousands upon thousands of these obviously spontaneous actions had a profound effect on how the Iraqis see us. They knew we did a lot of stupid and overbearing things, even brutal and criminal things at times. But they also could not deny that, on the whole, our people had a heart for them, or at least for their kids. And who couldn't like Iraqi kids? Practically everywhere the kids loved to see the soldiers, and the soldiers loved to see the kids.

War is ugly. But if you are going to fight at all, it's important to fight to win. We have created the conditions for peace in Iraq. But our job is not finished. The worst thing that could happen now would be surrendering when victory—real victory, not just empty triumph—is so close.

When our troops start drawing down, as they should when the conditions are favorable, the drawdown must be done methodically, for reasons both strategic and logistic. A hasty withdrawal would only empower our enemies and allow al Qaeda to regenerate. Politics dictates that politicians talk about withdrawal. The truth is right now we need more troops here, so we can get out of these tanks and other armor in Mosul and start walking the streets. The higher truth is that we are so close to winning, winning in the big sense of seeing Iraq be free and democratic, united and at peace (by local standards), that it would be a crime to hold back now. Maybe creating a powerful democracy in the Middle East was a foolish reason to go to war. Maybe it was never the reason we went to war. But it is within our grasp now and nearly all the hardest work has been done.

Whoever becomes our next president in January 2009 must be prepared for an uptick in violence in Iraq shortly after the inauguration. Insurgency is political war, waged on the news cycle, and our enemies might well try to create an illusion of strength. If the new president is panicked by an illusion and pulls our troops out, we and the Iraqis likely will pay the price for decades, perhaps generations to come. If we precipitously withdraw our troops, all of the tremendous progress we are seeing will be lost. The region could descend into chaos.

★ ★ ★

One of the saddest things about the Iraq War has been the political polarization back home. There is no doubt that it was an elective war and poorly executed. But some of our own countrymen want to see us lose this war. For many people it seems to be more important that they win the argument than for justice to prevail and Iraq be free. On the other hand, those who support the war must remember that critics were often right.

Without the critics we might never have made the great changes of 2007, and the war would be lost today.

Since December 2004, I have been with the combat soldiers all over Iraq. I have been on countless combat missions, patrols, and meetings, spoken to Americans of all ranks and to Iraqis with incredibly diverse backgrounds. I wanted our side to win, but knew that neither mindless cheerleading nor mindless pessimism would help.

We can win this war. And if we do, it will be a victory of the same magnitude as the fall of the Soviet Union. It will not be a victory for the Republican Party. It will not be a victory for America and Great Britain and others "against" Iraq. It will be a victory for freedom and justice. It will be a victory for Iraqis and for the world, and only then will it be a victory for us.

A stable, reasonably democratic, and friendly Arab country will have been established in the heart of the Middle East. Al Qaeda will have been defeated not only militarily but morally, rejected by the very Muslims they claim to represent.

We can win. But we can still lose.

And if we lose, Iraq will be the worst foreign policy disaster in our history. Imagine Vietnam, then multiply it by al Qaeda and Iran.

This book covered a time in which our men and women in Iraq changed the course of history. They did it against the odds, contrary to all expectations. The American combat soldier is responsible for this historic achievement. There are those who fought. And those who didn't. Our soldiers often said, "The military is at war. America is at the mall." It has been our soldiers' choice, but they saw it as their duty. And so they lived through